The Dark Side of the Light

"Beware of false prophets who come to you in sheep's clothing, but inwardly are ravenous wolves. You will know them by their fruits."

-   Matthew 7:15

Rosie Shalhoub

Dedication

I dedicate this book to my children so that they will always stand in the light and fight for what is right. And to my husband, Ross, who gave me the wings to fly and the courage to soar.

CONTENTS

Foreword

Sharina Star

I was more than thrilled and honored to write this foreword for Rosie when she presented this book to me for the very first time.

Rosie represents everything in the psychic industry I am so passionate about, and her story is one that represents everything I have always detested in the psychic world.

We have been friends for many, many years, and during that time, Rosie has always shown respect, courage, appreciation, spunk, and a zest for life that has always attracted me to her and her work.

I was proud to hold a spot for Rosie each week on my award-winning radio show that ran across the nation for 27 years. Her ideals, magnetism, and honesty are what my listeners found to love in her. Our sell-out psychic club shows and boat cruises were incredibly fun and enjoyable until sadly, Covid19 hit, and we have had to put them on hold for a while.

I applaud Rosie for speaking her truth within these pages, and I respect the message she is trying to achieve.

I have always seen in Rosie an incredibly funny, amazing, and smart businesswoman whose honesty and integrity have always been at the next level.

I wish her the best with this book, as she has my ultimate blessings.

Sharina Star

Author, Radio Announcer, Entertainer, Marriage Celebrant, Feng Shui Consultant, Intuitive Professional Counsellor, Hypnotist, Private Investigator, Profiler, Actress, TV Presenter & Volunteer Mentor at Frank Baxter Juvenile Detention Centre.

Preface

"Sharing the trials and turbulence of the deepest moments of our lives with others helps build a healing web for all."

- Dr Gulrukh Bala

I have been wanting to write this book for many years, and yet each time I would put my pen to paper, I would chicken out in the fear that the industry I am so passionate about would turn on me. It took me a long while to finally find the courage to sit down and let the words flow. Doing this became a real personal growth experience for me also, yet it has been confronting, to say the least, and I know that it is not going to make me many friends in the "spiritual" industry. Within the book, I use the word spiritual in inverted commas as sarcasm, as the industry itself is far from my understanding of spirituality.

Writing this has also been extremely cathartic and therapeutic. The more I found myself brutally honest and authentic, the more I felt liberated. No more hiding behind a fake façade of being nice in order not to hurt anybody's feelings. This book is all about my story, my thoughts, my experiences, and my truth. I urge you to keep in mind that my intention is not to incite hate, harassment, or revenge, and I apologize in advance if this is the way you see it. I can back up each and every story I speak about within this book with a source. I would also like you to treat this book as my own opinion, and my conclusions are the truth in the way I see what the truth to be. You may not agree with my opinions, and I respect that; however, I ask that we agree to disagree politely and with kindness, as I don't mind a good debate. I am sure that many of the people I speak about in this book may have started with good intentions, no matter how misguided and unethical their intentions actually are.

As you turn each page, I urge you to consider what you read as my opinion and as a criticism of how people in our industry make their money. I will never criticize anyone for giving things a go, making money ethically and morally. I love to see people succeed, but I need to insist that my issue is within the context of how they make their money. If you have taken what I say the wrong way, then you have totally misunderstood the context.

The whole wellness, spiritual, new age, crystal, psychic, and healing business has seen a massive boom and a huge growth within mainstream consumerism. With celebrities promoting these industries, social media hype, and trends, the influence on society has been phenomenal. In parts, it is great that people are becoming more conscious, but my problem is what goes unnoticed in this roaring business, what goes on behind the scenes, and the quick rich schemes from many of the "gurus." This does a lot more harm than good, and for that, we need to take some responsibility. I have firsthand witnessed psychic after psychics build their careers, their business, and their income from a flawed and dangerous disregard for reality.

Don't get me wrong, a part of me is still terrified, as I know the backlash from the bullying and nastiness that the psychic world holds. I want to be brave enough to share my story without always portraying myself in a positive light. It feels extremely empowering to do so and liberating that the truth be told. Once word got out amongst the industry that I was writing this book, the harassment started. Text messages, letters, and emails were sent to me from other psychics making threats to my life, my business, and my family. It only gave me more strength to do so and more courage to know that the truth must be told.

It was not that long ago when I started to experience the full force of what it was like to be burnt out within the industry. It became more and more draining to listen to people's problems when I had enough of my own at home. I was under pressure to perform at my peak each and every day whilst living my business at a high pace and my personal one at everybody else's. It was not until my body screamed out in pain and said, "No more!" that I finally stopped and listened. It was not the fast pace of my life that inhibited me from living my authentic self; it was the secrets I was hiding behind the scenes. They churned in my tummy until it became bloated and sick. My heart raced whenever I would hear how amazing a so-called psychic medium/healer was, knowing in full truth the falsehood of their careers and the money they were extorting from unsuspecting clients. Spending intimate time with these people, befriending them, and working with them, gave me the opportunity to see behind the veil and into the truth. The truth became a murky river; I tried to see through the other end, wanting to believe the haze and the mist will eventually fade away. It didn't; it became worse.

So instead, I needed to have a long hard look in the mirror, and as I did, I found myself transforming. In doing so, I feel that I have come out of the other side with a huge smile on my face and feeling more at peace than I have ever been. It was at that moment I knew I had a story to tell.

To the same extent, in writing this book, I wanted to have the same impact on others. I wanted to make a positive contribution, to have something to give back. My book will be worth its weight in gold if I can get my message out there in the hope that people will find their own power instead of giving it away to someone who is just as lost as they are. The psychic industry is just that – an industry. A $2.2 billion a year industry that, along with many other industries, contains its fair share of fakes, frauds, charlatans, fame whores and wannabes. Not everyone in the field is spiritual. In fact, from my own experiences, there have been more that are not than are.

My observations over the past 30 years have not been in vain, so I don't want you to get me wrong either. Working in the industry over these years, I have been blessed to meet some amazing, true to the earth and honest psychics. They all know who they are, and even though they are far and few between, their work and what they stand for reminds me of why I am doing all of this in the first place. I have been in a position to work with psychics in both Australia and across the globe, some incredibly talented people and some that are not so. Like a child who watches its peers and promises themselves not to be like that, I, too, found myself doing the same. I also know that there are many psychics around the globe who I have not yet had the pleasure of meeting, who, too, are what I like to call the real deal. These are the ones who are sending me virtual winks around the world, as I know they get my message and what I am trying to achieve. There are also the ones who will not take what I say offensively; instead, it will be those that yell the loudest who will have the most to hide.

In real life, I am a very honest person. I have always stood with integrity and strong moral ethics, and I have prided myself knowing that my business has been run in the same manner. No amount of untrue gossip, backstabbing, betrayal, or lies can change the person I truly am. With no rules or regulations in the industry, everyone is fair game, and that game can be manipulated by the strongest personalities, who know how to talk the talk but have no idea how to walk it. I believe in free speech, and of course, in order to cover my backside, I have changed the names and personalities. But that wouldn't really matter either, because sadly, names and faces might be different, but the stories remain the same.

I have always had a deep passion in my life to help people, mother them, and make the world around me a much better place. I tend to do this with humour and food. I also love nothing more than to see others succeed and thrive, and the satisfaction I receive in this is like winning the lotto but on steroids. I made it my mission to keep being kind and helpful towards others, even though they too, like many others before them, just might turn around and stab me in my back. I am OK with that, as my back stands tall in the field of poppies. I know who I am, and I fully understand the law of karma, attraction and destiny. What is mine is there for the taking, and what is yours is there too. I also understand the law of Oneness and that the God force is within all of us, which is why I do not enjoy competition or aggressiveness in order to succeed. I do so at my own time, at my own pace, and at my own game.

And, of course, I wanted to leave a legacy. I know I already started, but I also know there is much more to do before returning home to the pearly gates. If my words, my experiences, and life can help somebody else, then my job is done. I know that this book won't change the psychic industry overnight, but who knows, it might start making people have a good hard look at themselves and others, as I hope to leave an impact for many more years to come.

In the end, it will take enough good people to finally make things right in our industry, and I am lucky to know quite a few. Some I have worked with in the past, some I have never worked with at all, but that does not take away from the fact that they, too, like me, agree that it is time to stand up for the truth. As the great Voltaire himself once said, *"Every good man is guilty of all the good he did not do."*

Introduction

In a $2.2 billion-a-year industry, it is no wonder that anyone and everyone can be a psychic these days.

What makes it even more accessible is that almost no one is immune to the attraction and temptation of it all. The charm of finding instant answers to our most private and painful problems within 30 minutes, with a few flicks of the tarot cards, can become a seductive dance with a stranger who can tell you the answers that you want to hear. We have all been guilty of doing this at some level, including me, who classifies as a natural-born psychic.

I like to consider myself a highly intelligent and educated individual, but then again, so does everyone else. That leaves a huge gap in the industry for people to hand over their hard-earned money, even if deep down inside they know that there is a possibility the psychic could be a fake!

I was born in the year during which the hippie movement was in full swing. 1967 was the era of smoking pot and free-spirited flower children who were the future of our next generation. Free speech became the thing that was "in," women burnt their bras, and psychedelic mushrooms were ingested for breakfast, lunch, and dinner. Acid-induced paranoia that encouraged not only psychic phenomena but also schizophrenia left the population in a state of contradictions.

Shamans came out of the woodwork as Ayahuasca became a thing to do. Mystics found another way to make money. And some good money was to be had. Fast forward to today, the psychic "industry" is just that... an industry. A multi-billion, money-making, tax-evasion, lucrative cash market with no laws or regulations to hold it in place.

It wasn't always like that, though. In ancient times, seers and prophets were worshipped and adored. Only for things to turn around after the rule of Emperor Constantine in the early 300 A.Ds. Seers and prophets were then being burnt at the stake, persecuted in the name of God, becoming esteemed, and scorned at the same time. The psychics of the time, the real-deal seers, did most of their prophecies behind closed doors. They had to be very selective as to who they did their actual readings for.

So, let's take a walk down memory lane back to the

2

beginning of time, where we will have a look at how something so magically extraordinary has become so bastardised and corrupt in today's world.

Chapter 1

Early Seers and Prophets

So, where in the history of our time did psychics and mystics come from?

According to the trusty Wikipedia, *"A psychic is a person who claims to use extrasensory perception (ESP) to identify information hidden from the normal senses, particularly involving telepathy or clairvoyance, or who performs acts that are inexplicable by natural laws."*

The actual word itself goes back to a long time ago. From the ancient land of Greece and derived from the word "psychikos," which means "of the mind," it refers to the part of our mortal mind, or as some like to call it, our "psyche" or our "soul."

I am such a lover of Greek mythology, and, as we delve further into it, you will find that one of our favourite maidens, "Psyche," was known as the breath of the human soul. Like all ancient myths, her story is a tragic tale of love and betrayal, but it finishes with a happily ever after. However, her story is best left for another day and another book, but she became the epiphany of the word "psychic."

It wasn't until the 1800s that the French spiritualist and well-known astronomer, Camille Flammarion, gave rise to the word "psychic." From my understanding, he was the first person to have used the word, where it later became introduced into the English language.

Even though the word "psychic" itself is not that old, divination and fortune-telling go way back to ancient times.

It is accepted that in earlier civilisations, astrology was the most accepted form of fortune-telling. People only had to look up to the stars to predict the future and possible earthly events. The clever ones, however, didn't need to make predictions based on the placement of the planets. They were able to see "visions" and prophecies of the future. These people became known as seers, prophets, clairvoyants, or psychics.

In ancient times, these psychics, the ones who could see far into the future, had important leadership roles. They were high priests, judges, and advisors to the people of those times. You only need to open the pages of the Old Testament to see how prophets played a very important role in helping with the decision-making of the people in those days.

Both the Holy Bible and the Holy Koran mention Joseph, who would sit with the Pharaohs and interpret their dreams. He warned the Pharaoh that there would be eight good years, then eight bad years of famine. The Pharaoh, just like a psychic junkie, couldn't get enough of him.

Moses is the most important prophet in Judaism, according to the Hebrew Bible. The story says that he was an Egyptian prince who later turned into not only a religious leader and lawgiver but also a prophet. He was tuned into the laws of the Universe, so much so that Moses was able to lead the Exodus of the Israelites out of Egypt with the help of whatever supernatural force he had access to in those days. He parted the Red Sea and led his people to the other side, where he received the Ten Commandments.

Fast forward to the 21st century, and these Commandments are still very much relevant in today's world, as they were given thousands of years ago. The Hebrews have given the authorship of the Torah to Moses, who "channelled" that information just like any of today's writers.

And of course, none of us can forget the most famous story of all time. The one that included a family, all the animals on the Earth, a massive boat, a great flood, and the real reason why our planet has rainbows. Noah was given instructions to build an ark, and who was he to not listen to the word of the Lord?

We don't know for sure whether Abraham got his information from visions or dreams, but we do know that he was told to pack all his things up and leave his homeland. He was given the promise that he and his wife would be blessed with a family. The only problem was that Abraham was an old man, but he did what the voices in his head told him to do and found himself a much better life because of it.

Then, of course, we have the greatest prophets of all time, Jesus and Mohammed. I don't need to go into too much detail because I think you're getting the drift here.

I mean, the Bible has a whole Book of Revelations. An absolute massive chapter of doom and gloom for our modern-day world. It comes with its vivid imagery of disaster, suffering, and predictions about the end of the world. It is common knowledge that the "Devil's" number is 666, otherwise known in the Book of Revelations as the

"Mark of the Beast." Christians have always been puzzled about who this beast could be, yet scholars have come together to agree that simple numerology was in play at the time of that writing. I can't help but wonder if it was a smart way of getting a cryptic message across, using numerology as a sort of puzzle. After all, Nero was the Emperor at the time, and his name adds up to 666 in the Hebrew language. I suppose his persecution of Christians made him not so much of a nice guy after all.

Moving on from the world's three most influential religions, we go back in time to the Babylonians that worshipped the God Nabu. He was not only the deity of wisdom and learning but also prophecy. His name meant the "Announcer," which was about his prophetic and creative powers.

He was so clever that Nabu was adopted by the Assyrians and became known as the son of their God, Ashur. Even after the Assyrian empire fell around 612 BC, Nabu still managed to make his way into the 2nd century A.D., where he was worshipped still.

One of my favourite old-time stories is that of the Delphic Oracle. Not only is it the earliest story of classical antiquity but also of prophetic abilities. The Oracle of Delphi was an establishment in ancient Greece that was dedicated to none other than the God Apollo. Only one priestess was allowed to operate at Delphi, and the name given to her was Pythia. She had to give up her name and identity when she became a priestess. So much protocol, but obviously, the ancient Greeks took their prophecies to a whole new level.

Apollo's temple was at Delphi, somewhere on the slopes of Mount Parnassus in Greece. As the legend goes, the God would answer questions through the medium of His priestess, who ultimately became famous for her very ambiguous predictions made during frenzied states. The academics have suggested that too many volcanic gases were inhaled, which could have played a part in her strange mutterings or gibberish language. Now, I am no scholar, but I would probably place my bets that the latter could be true.

Either way, the priests at that time believed her voice to be Apollo's, which led the way for some of the greatest Greek literature this world has ever seen. The last recorded psychic message that was given at the Oracle happened in 393 A.D. when the emperor Theodosius the First ordered pagan temples to cease their operations. Some historians have even gone as far as to believe that Pythia spoke intelligently and gave prophecies in her voice. In any case, who are we to argue with a Greek priestess who was most probably high on ethylene gas?

The Seven Fires Prophecy

Now, let's discuss some of the gravest and serious prophecies that were told before us. These prophecies came during different eras to different people, but to our understanding, they can still hold. For example, let us consider the Seven Fires Prophecy. A prophecy told by the Anishinaabe people, it is considered to be warning us of the destruction humanity might face if we do not choose the spiritual path. The Anishinaabe people are tribes, and according to their stories, seven prophets came to them in the form of humans that had supernatural powers. They came from the ocean and glowed. Now what we need to know is that these Native tribes existed long before the Europeans migrated to North America.

According to them, the first prophets warned them about the "light-skinned race" that would bring death to their land. Sounds scary but, unfortunately, true. The next prophets warned them that this race would either bring

10

harmony and peace or destruction. According to the prophecies, we are in the seventh round currently, or era as referred to by the Anishinaabe people. The prophecy says that the light-skinned race shall give up materialistic views and join the path of spiritualism. That two more races would join them to bring world peace.

Hopi Prophecies

According to the Hopi people of the Native American tribes, many prophecies dictate the fate of the world. We have to see their tablet and rock pictographs to understand it all. Most of these prophecies that I found discuss the ending of the world or the emergence of the New World. Their most famous one is about a "Blue Star" that will appear and signify the emergence of the Fifth World.

Mother Shipton

An English woman named Ursula Southeil, who lived during 1488 and 1561, does not sound as important. But when I mention that she was famous throughout London for being a prophetess and soothsayer, she becomes ten times more interesting. Her predictions and prophecies were told similarly to Nostradamus, poems that could be interpreted personally. She made many famous predictions that preceded her lifetime, such as the Great Fire of London in 1666, modern technology, and the defeat of the Spanish Armada in 1588. The woman even predicted her death. Now that's a real psychic!

The Dooms Day Prophecy

Everyone loves a bit of a mysterious and scary doomsday prophecy. I have always been curious about when or how the world might end. However, we cannot leave one of the most popular doomsday prophecies out of the discussion. The world and everyone in it thought that the apocalypse was upon us in December of 2012. People chalked it up to the Mayan calendar, which consists of 144,000-day long cycles. When the calendar showed the ending of the 13th cycle, people thought it meant the end of the world. However, it was a heavily misinterpreted prophecy because Mayans predict that life goes on. What we need to understand is that no matter which ideology or religion predicts the end of the world, we have to admit our responsibility in the fact that we are driving this world to its very end.

White Buffalo Calf Woman

One great legend is of the White Buffalo Calf Woman from the Itazipcho Native tribe. Called Ptesan-Wi in Lakota, the White Buffalo Calf Woman came to the people when they were starving and needed guidance. She brought them the chanunpa, a pipe that is supposed to represent everything that grows on Earth. The prophet came to them, bringing wisdom and words of prophecy that could be interpreted by everyone their way. After she had visited the tribe, they received a hoard of buffaloes that helped them survive, and now the legend is passed through generations.

Russian Beliefs

In Russia, many things seem otherworldly, but nothing compares to the fact that you can get licensed as a magician or witch by the State. Yes, the government issues licenses for magical and psychic practices! The nation had a widespread belief in witches and psychics, but it wasn't always so. Due to the collapse of Communism, people were left with a void in place of a missing ideology. They turned to spiritual and psychic abilities to help guide them. However, due to Christianity spreading in earlier times, people were still burned at the stake for proclaiming themselves as psychics. Modern Russia has changed the perspective quite a lot by now, and seers or prophets are regarded with a lot of admiration.

Aboriginals

Aboriginal Australians have their spiritual and mystical experiences and beliefs. When diving into the beliefs, you will be attracted to the vagueness of it all. According to their beliefs and religion, The Dreamtime is the "unity of waking-life and dream-life," and it does not have a certain time or era that it happened in. It could refer to how the spirit began life and the Universe. Or it could mean the way of life, including how to live and pray.

Since time is abstract in their beliefs, they do not believe in an end or a beginning. The present and future, as well as the past, exist on the same plane, which is why many have a common belief that Aboriginals have psychic abilities. They believe that "dreaming" allows them to have knowledge of things to happen or that have already happened.

Orishas

There is another ethnic group that hails from Western Africa called Yoruba. Their religion is Santeria. Why do I mention them, you ask? Well, in their religion, there are Orishas that are the seven manifestations of the God Oludumare. Priestesses or priests can contact these spirits by dancing to drums and entering a trance-like state. These Orishas then enter their bodies and help with problems regarding human life. Now, let me tell you that even though people claim that there are around 400 Orishas, there are the main seven ones. These are considered "Seven African Powers" called Yemaya, Chango, Oya, Elegua, Obatala, Ogun, and Oshun. According to the tribe elders, these spirits are a combined strong force against any life's problems. Quite neat, huh?

Michael de Nostredame

Now, let us dive into what is the legend of the most popular psychic in modern times. Nostradamus was a French astrologer and psychic during the 1500s. He is most famous nowadays because of his book of prophecies. That book includes prophecies in the form of poems that he said he got through visions after staring into flames at night or pools of water or breathing in herbs that stimulate the brain. His prophecies were not specific to time or people, but people have interpreted them on their own a lot. Some believe he predicted events of our present-day world such as the atomic bombing of Hiroshima, the 9/11 attacks in the USA, floods, earthquakes, etc.

Spiritualism in the 1800s

When we talk about Spiritualism, we do not consider the impact it had on the world. The effects are still visible today because everywhere I go, I run into people that either believe in the afterlife and a way to contact it or in psychics. The wave of Spiritualism spread throughout America during the 1800s. It was called the Spiritualism wave because that is when psychics started using their powers to project themselves as a medium that could talk to the dead. Of course, that brought many people looking for advice and predictions of the future. This was when different factions of psychics started being formed, such as the New Age one. Spiritualism is why a lot of people believe in psychics nowadays, which allows them to be vulnerable to attacks from fake ones.

Edgar Cayce

After I have mentioned Nostradamus, someone that people consider a prophet, I cannot let Edgar Cayce go ignored. He is one of the most well-known psychics of our time. When I say that he was a psychic, I mean that he could do it all. As a psychic, we all have our abilities and niches, but he could almost do it all. Considered the modern Nostradamus, he made many predictions that came to be true. He even talked about reincarnation and would diagnose mysterious illnesses. He would go into a trance and start talking about future events. Being someone who loves a bit of mystical with a touch of fiction, I found out that he even talked about the possible existence of the famed underwater city of Atlantis.

Theosophical Society

The New Age brought many revolutions in the psychic world, but I want to talk about the theosophical society. Helena Petrovna Blavatsky founded it in 1875 in the heart of New York City. She founded it based on her journey of studying sages and oriental depts. The society was to form a circle of brotherhood that celebrated unity without discriminating against sex, race, caste, colour, or creed. They wanted to study science, philosophy, and comparative religion. They wanted to establish a society that could investigate the unexplained laws of nature and the powers of people.

The society that still exists today spent their time studying psychics around the world. With many investigations conducted on mystical and unexplained abilities, they helped lead the way for psychic studies. The New Age that began in the 70s was the era where different spiritual practices developed in the Western world. People could practice psychic and prophetic abilities in the open and learn about it even more.

New Age

The New Age movement grew popular in the 1970s. Though analytically regarded as religious, those people will rarely use the term New Age; those in the movement almost always prefer the designation "spiritual" or "spiritual body," while those outside the movement prefer "mind, body, and spirit." This anticipated "a New Age of Love and Light" and offered a glimpse of the future through personal and spiritual transformation. Gnosticism has been popular among adherents of modern esotericism in the West since the 2nd century. For Gnosticism was replaced by several esoteric movements in the 18th century, including the Rosicrucian Order and occultism in the 19th and 20th.

I could seriously babble on for pages here if I was to dig in deeper, but I just wanted to give you a brief rundown of how long psychics have been around. They say that prostitution is the oldest profession in the world, I reckon we psychics could give those sex workers a run for their money!

Psychics with Certificates

Speaking of certificates, there are "psychics," and I use that term loosely, who are now parading around as wellness coaches. They get certificates in the name of self-care and are swindling people out of thousands of dollars in the name of helping them connect with themselves. People are using "intuitive" abilities to help others unlock their potential and reach for greatness. With a thousand dollars a ticket, it seems more like a way to unlock another bank account rather than someone's intuitive abilities. These people are willing to provide common and basic advice in the name of psychic abilities to earn a name and money.

Chapter 2

The Land Beneath the Sea

"You can't cross the ocean of life just by dreaming about it; you have to jump in and swim."

- Debasish Mridha

As a child, I was always very intuitive. I would tend to know things that others wouldn't. I sensed things that were not physically accessible, and I was able to see things beyond the normal realm. I could talk to people who others could not see, and I saw colours and rings around people, animals, and plants. That I thought was just as normal as you see this book that you are holding in your hands right now.

I have not been the easiest person to understand, as my beliefs and experiences are very different from the ones that most people generally have. Sometimes I don't even understand myself, but I know what I know, and that is all I need to know.

Throughout life, I have been lucky enough to have supporting and loving people around me who have accepted me for who I am and the supernatural world in which I sometimes live. If lights were to ever go flickering or there were strange bumps in the night, you could almost guarantee that wherever I was, "they" would follow. Not many people liked to hear of my psychic experiences, and looking back, maybe it just spooked them out because I knew sure as hell that it freaked me out too!

During my childhood, I wasn't aware that my heightened senses and these experiences were beyond usual and not exactly what others would call 'normal.' For me to see somebody's aura or figures standing with them was quite normal, and I had no reason to question it as I guess I just assumed everybody else could see the same.

I was always an inquisitive child. I loved immersing myself in encyclopaedias and looking at the pretty colours of the crystals. I would collect rocks and seashells and felt certain energies from them that I didn't feel when they were not with me. My favourite place was the library or the book store. You could call me a bit of a bookworm, but I was definitely no nerd. I still remember my year three teacher asking us what we all wanted to be when we grew up. There was no question about it; I was going to be a famous movie star, living in the hills of Hollywood and adorned with all the jewels I so loved reading about. It wasn't until my friend Maria S turned to me and said, "Hey Rosie… you know if you become a movie star, then you will have to kiss so many different strange men!" It was then that my dream was shattered. There was no way I was ever going to receive any boy germs! It was there, in my grade three chair, I very quickly changed my career aspirations and decided to become more like my mother instead.

Some of my favourite memories of childhood would be my dad driving me to Dymocks, a book store in the heart of Sydney. He would take us there every Sunday, and I had the option of two levels of books that I could choose from. I was intrigued with anything and everything to do with crystals, magic, witches and warlocks, elves and goblins, and anything in between. My favourite series was the Chronicles of Narnia; I read a book a day over and over until my imagination, and my supernatural abilities all got lost into one. I would spend hours in the library with encyclopaedias and informative books. I loved researching different religions and schools of thought as I tried to make sense of the world.

I was always a popular kid, and I made friends very easily, but there were times when I was invited to a classmate's home, and I couldn't wait to get out of there. I could feel tension in the home, people who had passed on bugging me with messages that they wanted me to tell my mate's parents, and sometimes an eerie feeling that you get when you know something just isn't right. I got invited to all the parties; I was friends with everyone, and yet there were times where I enjoyed my own time. I would find myself during this space talking to my imaginary friends, meditating, and delving into deep thoughts and modes of relaxation; this would leave my mind in a state of subconsciousness so deep that I could see and hear essentially metaphysical things. I had a knack for becoming one with the elemental world where fairies and other kingdoms and dimensions were fun to play in.

My paternal grandfather was my favourite person to hang out with as a child. He loved indulging me in stories of his youthful days back in Lebanon.

My grandfather and I had a very settled routine together. He would drop me at school and then pick me up in the afternoons. Then we would head to Coogee beach, where I would share the details of my day while savouring our usual fish and chips. We would spend hours on the beach listening to each other's stories, and believe me when I tell you that my grandfather was some kind of storyteller! Perhaps I picked up my vivid imagination from him.

I enjoyed the stories of his younger days back in his hometown of Lebanon while he quite enjoyed my stories of the land beneath the sea. When I think about it now, I actually, despite being so young, knew a lot about places and things I had never personally witnessed or been to. For example, one afternoon, I related to my grandfather about these mysterious jewels and treasures worn in ancient times by elitist women in their prime. These women were to be found on an unknown island, where the economic system was such that no one had to suffer from poverty. It is only at a later stage in life that I realised I had unknowingly been speaking of the Lost City of Atlantis.

My grandfather was one of those old school and orthodox old men, but he would listen to my stories over and over and allowed what he thought was my rampant imagination to run wild. I can still hear his chuckle as I write these words and see his face vividly while the smell of our weekly fish and chips is wafting through my window.

I would always speak to him about magic, about times long ago where women were burnt at the stake and a mysterious island called Avalon. I instantly knew about witchcraft as though it had run through my DNA from generations before, and I told him how one day, in the future, the world would be very different.

I remember times when I would play with my imaginary friends and then narrate the stories to him. I would speak of my grandchildren like they existed, only to later realise that they were my grandchildren from a previous lifetime.

Despite never actually seeing a crystal, I knew all about them and also of the magic powers associated with them. I would insist with my grandfather that crystals had healing powers and that people are mostly unaware of how powerful they are. My grandfather would shake his head and smile.

I was about three years old when I had my first ever psychic experience. I remember it as clearly as if it was only yesterday. I was sleeping next to my mother, and I woke up with a scream and out of breath as I discussed the details of my dream with my mother. To her surprise, she had been having the exact same dream, and I remember it was the topic of conversation amongst her friends and family for weeks to come.

Looking back, so many memories come flooding in where I realise now that those moments were just not normal. On their return from Fiji, my parents had brought my sister and I signet rings, and I proudly showed mine off wherever I was. There was a day, however, that I had dropped it and my mother and I couldn't find it anywhere, although it fell from my fingers right in front of our eyes. It was as though it had disappeared into thin air during its fall. We searched high and low, inside and out, until we both knew it was time to give up, and my eight-year-old self-cried. I loved that ring so much with the two hearts that represented my parents, and I was devastated. My mum put me to bed, and I did not fall asleep; after all, it was still early in the afternoon. I cried and prayed and asked the "fairies" to bring it back. I knew exactly who had taken my ring, and I also knew my mother was outside hanging the clothes on the line when I felt a little bump by the side of my bed. I looked down, and just as quick as the ring had disappeared, it somehow magically reappeared out of thin air right by my side where I was lying. Mum obviously thought I was nuts, and when I tried to explain that the fairies had taken it, she wasn't having any of it. I was sad that I was the only one who could see the elementals as they brought me so much joy to play with as well as so much anxiety when they stole my things. After all, I, too, had an appetite for shiny, sparkly things, which has carried on fifty years later. There were times when I was routinely awakened during the dark of the night by "friends" who wanted me to come and play. I had no idea that these mates of mine were actually "dead" until my grandmother had taken me to a Tupperware party at one of her high society gatherings. I sometimes felt like the trophy child as her friends would ask me questions, and somehow, I would know the answers.

Obviously, at that age, I had no idea that I was a medium, and quite frankly, I had no idea what that word would have even meant. So, while my grandmother's friends were all gathered around the Tupperware table, I noticed the dark eyes of an Arabian sultan looking back at me. At eight years old, I thought he was old, but thinking back, he would have been no more than thirty years old. His English was not the best, but I could understand each word he said through his broken accent. There was something mysterious about him, and I was drawn to his energy. I felt like he was reading me like a book which made me feel uncomfortable in my young body, but I also felt like I had known this man from a distant past, thousands of years ago. Strange, huh?

I don't remember his name, but I still remember his face, and he asked if he could take my left hand, and he proceeded to read my palm. The Arabian prince, which is what he was in my eyes at the time, told me things he could not have possibly known and said that one day I too would be doing what he does and making lots of money from it. I had no idea what he was talking about, but he proceeded to tell my grandmother about a gift I was given and that I would one day be using it for the good of the world. He even told me that I would one day have a pigeon pair of twins, and they too had some pretty amazing things to do in this world. Fast forward to 2006 when Joey and Ellie were being born, and I felt the Arabian prince's breath on my face as I held my twins in my arms for the very first time.

When you are eight, these things don't really mean much to you, but when you get older, they begin to make sense. That man's eyes still pierce through my psyche, and I wish I could find him once again to say thank you.

Coming from a big fat Lebanese family, it is only natural that our get-togethers would consist of noise, lots of food, loud music, homemade alcohol, and of course, good coffee. And this is where an aunt, twice removed, married to a distant uncle related to my grandmother on her father's side, comes in. Aunt Therese taught me how to read the coffee cups. I couldn't wait for family luncheons to be over so we could get the Turkish coffee out and start reading. I learnt how to read the patterns in the cups and how to see the pictures and turn them into stories. She taught me to see into the future of the person sitting next to me through the granules of mere coffee beans, and she explained that it didn't matter what I would "see" as long as I trusted myself to say it out loud. I was blessed to be surrounded by people who encouraged my talent and who would enjoy the stories I had for them.

By the time I was a teenager, I had become outspoken about issues I found unjust in the world and rebellious to the Catholic Church which I was schooled in. It was one day in 1984 when Sister Bernadette made me get up in front of the whole classroom and apologise for my stance on gay marriage. This was never heard of back in those days, but I promised her that one day God would find a way for gays to be legally married, and the world will be OK with that. I even remember telling the class of '84 that "love is love" with so much pride (pun intended) and knowing that I was predicting something in our near future that the Catholic nuns were nowhere near ready to accept. And in doing so, Sister Bernadette did what any cranky, long-running nun married to the church's institution would do… she put me on detention!

I knew by the time I had graduated high school that I had a gift, a talent, a knack for knowing things before they had happened. I would always find my uncle sending me to the newsagent to fill in his lottery numbers. Somehow, we never won. On one occasion, when I was running one of his errands to the old-style bakery to buy cream puff apple turnovers, an old man had fallen. A crowd quickly gathered, and his body lay still. Everybody thought he was still alive until I literally saw his spirit stand in front of me, give me a wink, and with a flash disappeared into thin air. I told the people that he was dead, but what did I know? I was just a young teenager on her way back to eat fattening cream puffs with her uncle.

I believe my intuition saved me from situations growing up that could have got me into trouble otherwise. From getting "creepy" feelings about certain people to knowing not to go to a party I had been invited to, to instinctively knowing which friends I should hang out with in social circles, I had always felt surrounded by love around me, an angelic presence, so to speak. The Violet Flame became a companionship in my life that guided me to where I am today.

Growing up in a Catholic school, it was only quite obvious that the saviour we would learn about was Jesus Christ. I felt a strong connection with his work, I enjoyed reading the Bible, and I felt His energy around me at all times of my life. I would sometimes sit by the side of my bed and just chat with Him as I would with an old friend and ask Him to show me the way when I felt lost and alone. The Lord's

Prayer became entrenched into my veins, and even to this day, I will say it with conviction, faith, and sentiment. It wasn't until one day, lying in my bed, that the arm of Jesus came out of His picture, which hung above my bed. He laid His hand on my head and told me that he had some pretty important things that were needed from me. I asked Him if I could go with Him to the pearly gates, and His words forever etched into my soul told me that now is not the time for he had some very important things he needed me to do, and with that, He showed me a glimpse into my very own future where I saw myself helping people find their way in life in a very unusual and unconventional way for those times.

And so, I left my teenage years behind as I walked into the big wide workforce. I realised pretty quickly that the corporate world wasn't for me, and I yearned to work with my natural-born talent. It was many years later, where I sat with my first client, and it became the beginning of my lucrative psychic career.

It was a really calm spring night on September 11th, 2001. My little brother had just had surgery, so I decided to hang out at my parents' place with him for a few days and keep him company. Later that evening, I got into bed with him to watch a movie, and as we just got into it, the late news came on with a news flash that an aeroplane had hit one of the twin towers in New York. Mmmmmm, I looked at my brother and very casually told him that that was weird because I had a dream the night before about an aeroplane hitting a building. But in my dream, it was actually two planes and two buildings right next to each other. In real life, I had never heard of the twin towers, but yet the footage from our television screen was eerily familiar to where I had travelled in my dream. Not long after I mentioned this to my brother, another news flash let us know about another plane hitting another building. I looked at my brother with goosebumps covering my entire body, and he looked at me and, without hesitation, said, "Get out of my bed, you freak," as he called out to our parents to tell them what I had envisioned. I know I freaked him out that night, but it was nothing to how much I had freaked myself out.

Ever since that fateful night, my brother will always ring me with football tips or horse racing. Most of the time, I am right, but god forbid I make a bet for myself, and I can be guaranteed I lose out every single time. I must admit, one of my all-time favourite things to do is go to the pub with my brothers and sisters on Anzac Day. It is an all-time Australian tradition, and we play a game called "Two Up," which the soldiers invented in the war. It's quite simple really, the coin is tossed, and it is either heads or tails. Let's just say that each year my brother shouts us all out that evening for a meal at our local and favourite Chinese restaurant because I have never been wrong with his bets yet. The very second, however, I place my bets, I lose. I wonder why that is? I will never know.

Another Aussie tradition is the Melbourne Cup Day, a horse race held obviously in Melbourne and on the first Tuesday of November. Our whole nation stops still. It was about 5 years ago when I placed a bet on the Trifecta, and the winnings were something around $40,000. Me, along with two other psychic friends, guessed the first, second and third place, and we had won the race. However, as the law of no-no's go in the psychic world would have it, I didn't pay for the bet properly, and of course, we all took home nothing that day. I knew the Universe was playing with me, and I just smiled, shook my head, and promised never to bet again. As a sidenote here, I no longer advocate betting on the horse races, as I have now come to educate myself on the cruelty of the horses and their treatment before and after the races. No wonder the Universe was steering me in another direction, as there was no way I would have ever morally enjoyed that money. I did feel bad for my friends, though, as the power of three once again proved to be an almighty force.

Naturally, the question has to be asked, "Is being a psychic the right way to earn a living?" Of course, I am going to be biased and say yes, but my yes depends on whether you are a naturally born hundred per cent fair dinkum, runs through your veins type of psychic, or whether you are a textbook kind of psychic. And just like in all types of industries, there are what you call the wannabes, the try-hard, the fame whores, and God forbid the fakes!

Chapter 3

She's Got Balls!

"Sometimes it takes balls to be a woman."

From Christmas balls to crystal balls, I am still in awe of how I managed to create two thriving businesses with a little help of balls! I am a psychic by nature. I can see beyond the natural realm and can communicate with Spirit. I have always had a strong connection with crystals, even before I knew of their healing properties.

I believe with my heart and soul that we are all born with a God-given gift or talent, and we must use it in our lives to find our happiness and wealth. Since I was a little girl, I have always wanted to be on the stage as I absolutely love theatre, and when the cast is taking their final bow, I sometimes wish to be up there joining them before the curtains close. Growing up, we lived next door to an actress who would take me to the Channel 9 T.V. studio with her. I would be in awe as the actors and actresses would get dressed up, fussing over with makeup and hair. She was married to the CEO of the Regent Theatre, in the heart of Sydney city, and I would have access to the backstage where I sat behind the curtain dreaming of my future on the stage.

I cannot sing, I will never be able to sing, and no matter how many singing lessons I may have, I will never sing, so it is only obvious that I was never destined to be on the stage. My father was a professional musician in his younger days, and I clearly remember going to music studios with him for recordings and sitting in awe, wishing I could be more like him. He even taught singing, guitar and piano lessons a few nights of the week, and yet, very sadly, I did not inherit one ounce of his talent.

I also wasn't given the gift of being mathematically competent either. No matter how hard I try, two plus two will never equal four, so finding a job in a field that requires numbers was never going to be for me either. My store, Embrace, always looks aesthetically pleasing and stunningly beautiful, but I can never credit for that as I just don't have a good eye for merchandising. When stock comes in, all I see is boxes and mess everywhere. My girls, Angelina and Lara, however, have this knack to put it all together as if they have just waved a magic wand, and they make it look uber amazing. You see, we all have a talent, and I believe that there is nothing wrong with making money and a great career with our gifts.

I am very creative and have always been a great artist, which led the way to Santa's Little Painters becoming a hugely successful business for me and one that I had just fallen into without really trying. On top of that, with my ability to see into the world of psychic phenomena, it only made sense that I created a career on the talents I was naturally given at birth.

It frustrates me like crazy when I see people trying to be something they are not and, in doing so, missing out on their rights to be something amazing if only they could tap into their given gifts. My husband, Ross, has an uncanny way of putting colours together, and he has the job in our household when it comes to any interior design. This is not my forte, so he will forever be the leading person in our home to work out what goes where and if this goes with that. You should be getting my drift here, and with that said, I truly do not believe that anybody and everybody can just become a psychic. Just as I will never be singing my lungs out to 'Don't Cry for Me, Argentina' on Broadway, so too, you won't be a psychic if it is just not a part of your genius zone.

While I initially used to be an active part of the family business, I knew instinctively that I had something a bit more to offer the world. I learned how to make money from my father, and I also learned how to run successful businesses. I had the perfect base to start my entrepreneurial finesse and the best teacher in the world for it.

I knew that at some point over the next few years, it was my destiny to make an entry into the industry of psychics and combine it somehow with my artistic talent. I wasn't quite sold on the how as yet, but I knew it was a given and something I needed to follow the signs with. Sadly, in the millennial age, the psychic world has become an industry. This is an entire field that is not governed by laws and regulations. It is filled with cash in hand transactions and loads of people willing to take your dollars in need of you by giving a glimmer of hope.

In the early '90s, I had a dream in which a beautiful blonde woman with a white cloak came to me and told me to start importing Christmas decorations and setting up sites that would soon become franchises in multiple shopping centres. Who was I to question what I believed to be my spirit guide? I found myself researching and figuring out that there was an untapped niche due to seasonal demand. With that, I started what years later became a successful multi-million-dollar business. Santa's Little Painter's was born, and as I was personalising baubles for customers, I also received psychic messages to relay back to them.

As was the case of my Christmas business, I started Embrace when I received divine guidance to do so. I had a magnificent dream in which I was seated in a room full of crystal orbs that shone like diamonds in the glistening light. The same lady that had appeared in my previous dreams walked up to me and asked me to follow her into a room at the back where shelves filled with crystal orbs of all sizes covered the walls, and in the centre, there was a huge crystal ball, the size of a baby whale. She spread her arms a foot above this orb and held the position for a few minutes; the lights flickered, and the air seemed to become still. Then, a light was emitted from within the crystal ball. Soon I could see myself within the crystal, standing in a shop similar to the one outside, dealing with clients, reading tarot cards and indulging in crystal gazing.

The lady who showed me the vision within the magical sphere quietly spoke to me and said, "You are a seer." I responded in the affirmative, and she said, "Reach out to people and use your abilities to serve. There is no better virtue than to help the ones who can't see." At first, I nodded, accepting her statement at face value, but then I realised that I didn't know how to act upon her advice, so I questioned her, "How do I reach out to the people?

People who have passed on approach me themselves, while people mostly cringe at the mention of magic and insight. The woman gave me a comforting smile and said, "The opportunity will come to you itself; you just need to be open to receiving. Also, remember; always attach a price to your powers. What has value should be held in the same esteem; people only value that which comes at a price." No sooner had she said this, the emission of light from the globe dulled. Once again, the lights flickered, and slowly the woman and the room began to blur.

I awakened in my room to find silver moonlight washing over my bare arms. I was startled by what I had seen, but the memory of my dream was so vivid that I knew it had to mean something. I concluded that the time had come for me to make the most of my psychic capabilities, and so I started exploring my options.

It was early in the '90s when one day, I wandered into an exquisite new age shop. I roamed the shop and found myself drinking in the interior of the shop and its contents. It was an exceptionally satisfying experience for a soul like mine. Walking through the aisles, the crystals in the store filled my senses, and I felt at home.

The shop had a room at the back, which intrigued me, especially since I had seen a dream with regards to such a room. I walked towards it and entered in awe, for it was indeed filled with crystal orbs, just like in my dream. I stood rooted to the spot, staring at the huge glass orb in the centre. I thought of doing some crystal gazing but wondered whether the policies of the shop would allow me to sample their wares in such a manner. As I turned to head out and ask at the counter, I saw a woman walk through a pair of curtains on the right that I had not noticed earlier. My jaw dropped. She was the same lady who was in my dream. She walked towards me and gave me the same eerie smile that I instantly recognised from my dream. "I did not need to wait for you with much impatience, Rosie, for I had already 'seen' that you will join us soon," she said, with emphasis on the word 'seen.' I spoke with a conviction that was unknown to me, "I too had 'seen' and it is indeed a pleasure to be here. How soon can I join?"

I joined the shop and went on to become like the fabric of the shop. This was my first experience of working on something so spiritual.

I made many friends at the shop, which included other employees in the store, as well as clients. To me, this was the world of spirituality, and everything was bound to be pure. It's the people that count the most. There was an Italian employee that I befriended who was a very genuine soul. She had seeing capabilities that made me feel like a pea in comparison.

Maria would adore me, and I really looked up to her too. She especially inspired me because of her ability to meditate and then come back to the present with more knowledge of the past or the future. Like me, she too could see into previous lives. We shared a special bond even though she was much older than me, and our friendship extended beyond the workplace. One day while she was at the crystal orb, she saw that I was following in her footsteps, and she instinctively knew that I would be taking up her position as the main psychic at the store. A few months later, she fell sick and left the shop, and I took her place. I worked at the shop for three years.

In my initial years, I felt that anyone who could see would know that the world beyond requires one to be most honest and simple at heart. Boy, was I wrong! It was my perception that our field was one with high levels of love, purity, morality and conscientiousness. However, I soon came to learn through personal experiences with people that, in reality, even the world of psychics is contaminated by jealousy, spite, maliciousness, and above all, dishonesty, deception, and a whole lot of nastiness. Over the years, I saw firsthand that many people were just impersonating psychics or healers in order to exploit people by making them believe that they had the insight and the ability to help.

A few experiences come back to my mind. The gist is that others in the field would get jealous of a psychic if their name started to become well known. While a bit of jealousy may still be normal, I had never thought that people could be so mean and spiteful. After all, I was still a rookie and a young one at that; my rose-coloured glasses tinted my world.

Have you ever just adored someone, and then you become devastated to know that, behind your back, they are trying to malign and defame you by spreading a very hurtful rumour? As my reputation as a reader became more and more popular, my relationship with Maria began to sour. All of a sudden, she had created an entirely false persona that revolved around me being someone who was into dark energies and black magic. I felt sick when the rumours came back to me, and I just wanted to cry. My beautiful, lovely friend, Maria, who I looked up to with so much pride all of a sudden, had become my competitor. I was hurt, I felt betrayed, and yet I still loved this woman as an elder sister who had taught me so much, and she was still an ideal in my eyes.

I didn't know what to do once she stopped talking to me. My phone calls stopped getting answered. She made sure that our shifts at work did not clash in order to not bump into me, and the gossip started to get worse. My "friends," my girls who I used to hang with every day, started to become nasty towards me as I struggled to understand what I had done wrong.

I thought that sending Maria flowers with a beautiful letter of how I was feeling and how much she meant to me might help soften her and that she might see some reason behind this vendetta she had created for me. A week passed after the flowers were delivered and still no word from Maria. I was told that my shifts were being cut short in the store because the water in the vase in which Maria had the bouquet, started to go murky. Apparently, this was a sign that I was a dark witch and no logic was going to get through to any of the staff, or especially to Maria, that it is only normal after a week of being in a vase that the water would go a cloudy brown hue.

And so, I experienced my first taste of jealousy, maliciousness, and spitefulness. Staff turned on me and believed every word Maria told them about me. Little old Maria, butter wouldn't melt in her mouth, but instead, fire and brimstone came out of it with a vengeance, and I bore the full brunt of it.

Sadly, I did not know how to defend myself, and I felt lost, alone and confused. After all, I was working in the field of spirituality, and if I didn't have Maria to turn to for advice, then who would I turn to? And just like that, along came Helen.

Helen was a much older psychic and a very good one at that. I didn't really see her much in the store as our days and roster never seemed to match up. Helen, too, had heard the rumours of my broom riding and spell casting hearsay, and so she felt it time to take me aside and have a chat. And have a chat we did, and four hours later, I felt like I could walk on water. She comforted me enduringly by telling me how she could see how wrong Maria was in spreading the fake gossip about me, and she very sternly warned me of the illusions of the industry and that I had to learn to grow a set of balls if I wanted to continue doing this work. Helen gave me some protection tips on how to keep my energetic field clean and filtered, and not allow the negativity around me to get in. She also told me that in life, the only reason people say they have your back is so they can stab you in it the minute your back is turned. She gave me a two-hour lecture on discernment and how to work out the good from the bad eggs—her words sunk in deep.

Kissing her goodbye with gratitude and thanks, we exchanged phone numbers, and this became the beginning of a lifelong friendship. I very quickly adopted her as my grandmother and my fairy godmother. She became my spiritual advisor, my mentor, and she was always positively brimming with wisdom. I needed to believe in people, and yet I knew I was going to have to take off my glasses that were covered in roses in order for me to truly see.

I didn't realise until looking back how the dark was just as important as the light in everything we do in life. Darkness taught me how powerful the light is, it taught me about the yin and the yang, and it taught me to see the Star Wars movies in a whole new light. I didn't want to admit it at the time but, over the years, I came to realise that there really was a bit of Darth Vader in all of us. I don't know how I have done it, but I always seemed to have put myself in the right place at the right times. Even during the darkness, the light came to me in unusual and mysterious ways, and that included people I was blessed to have met during my journey.

I was introduced to Janine through my sister Michelle, who were both office workers in the same company, making their way up the corporate ladder. Michelle thought it would be a good idea for me to meet Janine as she too was into all the same weird stuff that I was into, and at a formal function, we finally met. Janine was not dressed like a witch, nor did she portray to be one, and yet, just like any good witch of the south, she was powerful beyond belief and capable of some magnificent spell casting I had ever seen. Instantly I took a liking to her, and I admired the way she knew how powerful she really was and yet didn't need to push it on anyone or show off about her status. She kept very quiet in the public eye regarding who she really was and carried on her days like the rest of us would.

Straight away, I knew we were soul sisters, fighting the galaxy with all its imperfections, and together we became a mighty force. All of a sudden, Friday night women's circles replaced watching re-runs of Seinfeld.

It was here within the circle that I became initiated into priestess, yet it took me a long time to realise the power I had as one and what I needed to do with it. Once our circle was open, I felt the immediate devotion to the goddess, and I related to the struggles and burdens she had to endure to become the mighty warrior. Each week we took turns to open the four directions and invoke the goddess into our sacred space. For me, this was my time of reflection, meditation and prayer. And afterwards, we celebrated with a glass of wine, cake and lots of sugary sweets. Friday nights couldn't come around fast enough, and I found myself amongst my homies, with hooded cloaks as we sang our praises to mother Earth and felt through our veins the ancient crones coming out in all of us. Even though I was still a young maiden at the time, my knowledge and thirst for more familiarity was turning me into a wise woman who could feel the blood of my ancestral witches running through my veins. It was during our circles where my mind opened up, and my third eye exploded with so much vision for the future that every time I did a reading for a client, I even blew myself away with the accuracy that I was speaking. Friday night circles became more than just a group of witches burning flames in a cauldron and honouring the full moon in all her glory. It became a place where I had finally found my sisters. It was a place where I was safe to be myself, where we told our secrets with no judgement, and I knew my back would always be covered by the women who nurtured and honoured each other. Janine taught me how to use herbs in sacred ceremonies, and as she had taken me under her wing, I found the biggest magic in my life was truly the power that, as a circle, we were able to generate.

Becoming a high priestess didn't come easily. It meant that I now had to use my inner strength to conjure up some of the most powerful manifestations I could possibly accomplish. It wasn't always easy, and it took more than just a wrinkle of the nose to make things happen.

Fast forward to 2010 when I opened Embrace in Westfield Miranda. Probably to date, one of the busiest shopping centres in the Eastern hemisphere, it was not only classy and modern, but it was also fun and enchanting. With hard work, lots of love, and passion, and with the right people by my side, it grew and developed into one of the best crystal shops in the country. Embrace quickly became known Australia wide, and it wasn't long after the world was knocking at our door. With my knowledge of business and my passion for turning my talents into money, Embrace became a household name.

I not only immersed myself in my craft, I was making a decent dollar doing it the spiritual way. I knew in order for Embrace to be different, it needed to make a stand, and at all cost's honesty, integrity, and strong ethics would be upheld at all times. Well, at least on my end, it did.

I gathered up psychics I knew were the real deal as by this stage, and with the internet and social media, it seemed that everyone and anyone was a psychic. Both my adopted grandmother and elder sister, Janine, became part of the fabric in the shop, and its family-based environment meant it was a place where nobody wanted to go home. I was in my element, we were making some good money, and I had my friends by my side to do it with.

It was here in 2010, within months of our opening, in walked Colin. An Asian man born in Hong Kong, he was all dressed in black, and I immediately noticed a huge, and I mean HUGE white glow around him. In fact, I actually felt him walk in before I saw him do so. His energy was so strong that I found myself being pulled closer and closer until both our arms opened wide and found ourselves in a massive embrace as if we hadn't seen each other for years. I guess, in my language, you could say we hadn't seen each other in thousands of years, but our energies resonated, and we both knew this was going to be the beginning of a very special bond.

It wasn't long before I nicknamed Colin "Mr. Miyagi," as I had my very own guide in just the same way Daniel Son had. Painstakingly, Mr. Miyagi taught me to practically wax on and wax off, and I questioned on many occasions whether he was truly human or not.

You see, my adopted grandmother, Helen, became my voice of reason, Janine, my teacher, and Colin...well, Colin was just like my guardian angel slash mentor slash magician slash karate instructor. The latter at which I failed miserably.

With Mr. Miyagi by my side, I learned about Chinese medicine, herbs and healing. We sat for hours and still do, discussing the wonders of the Universe and the true meaning of life. Philosophy, at its finest, is what I would always find whenever I was in Colin's presence.

It was here, with Colin, I learnt the secrets to manifesting. I learnt how to follow the signs to my next achievements and also the signs to keep me away from menace. He became very protective of me, and I saw in him a lion's roar that was louder than any other king of the jungle I had ever known. Except it wasn't a roar that could be heard with the ears, it was something that could only be felt and directed to anyone he felt was coming from the dark. Colin would always talk to me in riddles, and he would always say that many secrets are hidden in the dark. I always knew that he was referring to certain psychics I had working with me at the time; I just didn't know how much his words would ring true until many years later.

Colin would always warn me about the dark side of the light and how I had to be very careful because my light was so bright that people would use and abuse my kindness and goodness for their personal gain. He watched, he listened, but he did not speak and instead opened the door in the hope that I would understand the riddle in order to find the answer. Colin took me on long drives far and wide where we sat on rocks and looked at trees and meditated in Temples until I had an answer. The only problem was that I did not know the question.

Chapter 4

For Those Who Have Eyes to See

"Those that yell the loudest have the most to hide."

So, let's get one thing straight…just because somebody is a psychic, it does not automatically put them in the spiritual club. There is a massive misconception out there; people seem to think that a psychic is a very spiritual person because of the things they can do, see and hear. Nothing can be further from the truth, and it took me a long time to learn that psychic abilities do not discriminate or belong to a whole heap of mung bean-eating monks, meditating on a hilltop while chanting 'Om' all day and namaste-ing everyone who passed by.

As usual, Colin would always walk into Embrace at the moment I would need him the most. He taught me how to enjoy the journey, look out for the signs, and that there are never any ordinary moments, especially when I needed to keep my guard up against all the people who couldn't be loyal towards me or Embrace when opportunities for them arose. He had this knack of knowing who I should have working with me and who I should not, and just like any failing student, I had to learn the hard way when he marked my exams with a big fat F minus!

To this day, I never believed that Colin was truly human. As crazy as it sounds, whenever I was with him, I saw things manifest out of nowhere, and miracles happened that can't be explained even if I were to try. The more time I spent with Colin and the more I knew what he taught me, the more I knew that I actually didn't know anything at all.

And just as my adopted grandmother, Helen, would always tell me to trust my gut as it knew what my head hadn't worked out, I still struggled to learn that not every psychic could be trusted. So, my gut and my head would do a merry dance until I had the King and Queen eventually tell me, "I told you so."

In Embrace's early days, we offered psychic development workshops. Our classes would fill quickly, and I always made sure that breaks consisted of huge platters of gourmet sandwiches, lots of sugary treats along with tea and coffee. It was way too hard for me to teach these classes myself as my twins were only four years old at the time, and I was working hard on the backend of the store. We decorated the work table for the students with flowers and crystals and had the fairy lights and candles flickering in the background to create a surreal and gentle atmosphere. Our classes became ever so popular, and I believed that I had chosen well for the teachers representing Embrace's classes. It was a wet and windy Wednesday night where all the 'W's matched up, and in walked Wendy. She was a stunning brown-haired woman who stood regally and was dressed in the most exquisite caftan I had ever seen. Wendy so badly wanted to learn the tarot, and even though some weeks her train was running a bit late, she never missed a class. She would proudly take her homework home and learn her stuff but somehow never really grasped it.

During this time, Wendy spent a lot of money at Embrace on all sorts of different tarot decks, crystals, and anything in between that would help her enhance her psychic skills. Her spending had got to a point where we needed to take her aside and gently tell her that we didn't feel right taking so much money on the products she was buying. I spoke to the teacher of the class, and together we felt that Wendy just didn't have what it took to be the psychic that she so badly wanted to be. I spoke to Colin about it as I was starting to feel quite uncomfortable about the amount of money that Wendy was spending with us and that she had enrolled herself in absolutely every workshop we had to offer. Before I go on, let's go back to my longing to be on the stage…it is like a singing teacher continuing to take my money when she knows there is no way on this earth that I will ever become a good singer. And so, it was something like this, and Colin, who always had some words of wisdom, turned to me and said: "Rosie, this gift is only for those who have eyes to see, ears to hear, and hearts to fill." I asked him how this applied to Wendy, and he sat me down and told me another one of his famous parables, and my homework that night was to go home, open my Bible, and read Matthew 13:16-17. It was at that moment I knew exactly what he was getting at.

"For truly I say to you, many prophets and righteous people longed to see what you see, and did not see it, and to hear what you hear and did not hear it." I closed my eyes that

58

night with comfort in my heart, knowing clearly what I needed to say to Wendy the following evening. She was always going to be more than welcome to join us in class, but we did not feel that reading cards as a profession was a great new career move for her, especially because she was making things up as she went along.

We really did try to break it to her gently and point out that we think she should focus on what her true talent was, which was, of all things singing.

The following week we did not see Wendy in class, and I started to get this sick feeling in my stomach that maybe we had offended her, which was never the intention. She did not answer any of my calls when I tried to check in on her. Before even two months had passed, I walked past the psychic reading room at a well-established psychic fair only to find Wendy, deck in hand, giving a very young girl a psychic reading and giving her advice that would make this child's mother cringe. That weekend I heard that Wendy walked away with just a little over $1000 cash in hand for telling people what they wanted to hear, and I held my head down in shame. There are ways to make money, and then there are some decent ways to make money.

Sadly, Wendy wasn't the first, and she definitely isn't the last. Thessina walked into Embrace in its early years, asking for a deck of tarot cards that she could take home to learn how to read. As usual, I always recommend the Rider Waite as they were not only the original tarot written in 1910 but also because I find them the easiest to learn from. Thessina walked away proud of her purchase, and I kid you not, a week later, she proudly boasted not only a $500 an hour psychic reading with none only but Thessina herself, but also that she had been reading tarot her whole life and her gift was handed down from ancestors on her mother's side which made her a 6th generation psychic. Yeah – right!

Wendy and Thessina were never going to be the only ones who portrayed to be psychics and yet had no psychic ability about them. Many came and left just as quick, and as usual, they would all end up in the same circle of friendships that consisted of malicious gossip about one another filled with so much hate and spite and consumed with the green-eyed monster because nobody should dare become more psychic than they! The sad thing is that as the owner of Embrace, I got to hear it all from both sides as I watched them pretend to love each other when they thought that nobody was watching.

An empath like me, who is a bit of straight-one-eighty, I can't be around people like this for too long. Integrity means nothing to them. As I worked my way to where I wanted to go, as I found the bottom was too crowded with all their bitterness, I came to understand that their poison could tear any tall poppy down and damage them emotionally, spiritually and financially.

Helen would always tell me that happiness is not what you get; it is what you become and that staying in the present would help me see more into the future. Our weekly phone calls got more and more frequent as I poured my heart out on the injustices of these "spiritual" people. It was a Thursday morning, and I was just dropping the kids to school when Helen called me urgently as she needed to see me. I drove through the morning traffic, terrified that she was going to give me some bad news about her health. At 82, she was doing well; in fact, I questioned if she was actually fitter than me because she sure is a lot smarter and wiser than I would ever be.

I drove into her driveway, where she was waiting, her frail body recovering from hip surgery. She got into my car, and she took me to lunch. Champagne and seafood on the wharf were on the menu, and my adopted grandmother finally came clean as to why the meeting that day was so urgent. She had been given a vision, and it couldn't wait. Her words sunk in my veins as she told me I had to be careful of who I was going to share my weaknesses with because it will be many years later, when the opportunity presents itself, that they will use it against me. I knew Helen was referring to one of my staff, and deep down, I knew who she was talking about, but I also did not want to believe it. You see, sisterhood to me meant that each other's successes would be celebrated in order for us to lift each other high and inspire one another. That's what girls do, right?

Even though Helen was in her 80s with no children of her own, she too had adopted me as her granddaughter, but there was one thing that held us together over the 30 years we had known each other, and that was our friendship. A huge age gap between us, and yet our sisterhood held us together like two peas in a pod.

I was guilty of falling into the trap of believing that every woman who worked for me or became my friend fell straight under the sisterhood category. I cannot tell you how common it is amongst female psychics to hear them say to each other, "you are my sister." However, what I have experienced is that everyone is your sister while you are at their level. The game changes once your success exceeds theirs, and it becomes more like a game of snakes in the grass, and you quickly become demoted from sister to the second cousin twice removed.

You see, sadly in life, mediocrity attacks excellence, and I had never seen it more rampant than in the "spiritual" industry. However, what people, or should I say "psychics," never realised is that there were many times I had to fail on my way to greatness. Success comes with many holes in the ground, and it takes a long while to navigate them, so you don't fall in. There were times when I made a business decision so big that I truly thought it could have ruined Embrace when the outcome was nowhere near what I had perceived it to be. I failed on so many occasions, and it was my persistence, my faith in myself, and the teachings of Helen and Colin that got me back on my feet. They also taught me about discernment, the law of attraction at a much deeper level than I had ever known, and nothing that the textbooks or google could prepare me for. With these two allies by my side, I was a quick learning student, although at times, I failed a little.

I like to think of myself as a spiritual person, but yet I possess qualities that come with being human, and I have no qualms admitting this. I know my strengths, and I know my weaknesses, and I am not afraid to admit that at times the latter can overshadow all the good I have achieved. I am the first person to stand up and say, "Hey, you know what, I am not perfect, I have my faults, and yet I will continue to be the best person I can be." And this then brings me to the subject of gurus.

Sometimes things are not always what they seem, and people are not who they portray themselves to be. It took a lot of letdowns and disappointments for me to really grasp this, but even Colin would remind me that we don't always see what is right in front of us. This reminds me of a well-known international author I took on as a spiritual guru. I hung onto every word in her books, and I practised her teachings on a daily basis. Each time she visited Australia, I would stand in praise when she walked onto the stage and cry happy tears at being in the same room as her. A few years later, I got to know her personally and was fortunate enough to have been given the opportunity to work with her. When I use the word 'fortunate' here, it is because I was given a chance to fully open my eyes to the world of make-belief and false heroes.

Preaching over the years on the law of attraction and how to manifest anything you want in your life, I thought this woman was an enigma until one night, whilst working at the back of the stage, I saw firsthand what Colin was trying to warn me about all this time. She most definitely put on a performance of her life, and it concluded with a standing ovation from the crowd. I felt chuffed that I was chosen to work with this all-important woman until she came flying through the back curtain and, in a demeaning manner, demanded her assistant to get her a drink. I am not referring to water here either, as she needed something a little stiffer. I mentioned how her talk was amazing, and I will never forget the look in her eyes when she turned to me with a gaze and said, "Darling, if only I can believe my own bullshit, then everything would be perfect." She looked me up and down and said, "You are the psychic; you tell me when the love of my life is going to come?"

I cannot express how deflated I felt after that conversation as she laughed at her excited crowd still echoing from the auditorium and claiming how she had them all fooled. When I got home that night, I packed away all her books and put them out for the garbage collection. I felt numbness like I had just been blindsided by a big massive truck! Only recently, I saw this woman in an interview with someone we all might know; I felt sick. As she spoke about bringing love into your life and how everything can be perfect if you just let it be, the visions of her whisky in one hand and her drunken slur on romance as she fell off her chair will be etched in my memory like a thousand-year-old fossil hiding in the rocks.

Another well-known journalist I worked with for twelve months was not much better. Book after book, she had written on how to have a happy life, and yet hers seemed to be always in a constant state of doom and gloom. So much so that she let us down at the eleventh hour when we booked a whole auditorium of people to come and listen to her talk about a wonderful life. I never did get an apology nor an explanation other than that she had a fight with her boyfriend that night and couldn't perform on stage. We received strict instructions to tell her waiting fans that she was not well and nothing else, but boy, was it hard delivering the news to her eager fans and even harder to refund the thousands of dollars they had paid. We never heard from her ever again after that day. Since then, I refused to sell her books in my store out of principle, and I am still waiting for a polite apology, but I guess she is too busy working the stage preaching to the masses on how to live their best lives!

I long lost my need to have a guru in my life or even a hero. Time after time, I hear Colin's words in the back of my head, reminding me that this work is for those who have eyes to see and ears to hear, and I realise that we all see and hear what it is we want to. All these so-called gurus have an agenda and are not afraid to use it for their own benefit. If it doesn't suit them, then Sayōnara baby. For these guys, once they lose integrity, then the rest is easy.

Even I, the most sceptical psychic out there, have been fooled on occasions by other psychics. Lord knows I had them working for me at Embrace until their true colours came through, but the biggest sucker was me on a hot San Francisco summer day. I was on holidays with my husband Ross, and I thought it would be cool to check out the millions of billions of psychic readers they have on almost every street corner. However, we found Dalia in a cute little hideaway tucked behind some quaint old shops, and Ross thought it fun to shout me a reading as Dalia had come highly recommended by some random person he had met on the streets of San Francisco.

This is the perfect example where you know something isn't fitting in, but yet, you so want it to, so you just go with the flow anyway. The first thing I noticed is the half-filled baby bottle sitting on Dalia's reading table. I thought it a bit strange that her sacred space was not treated as such, and as I looked further around, I noticed a baby's pacifier on the floor and a half-eaten sandwich. Weird, I thought, as my attention went straight to her back door, which was piled with boxes upon boxes of rubbish that instantly gave her room a negative feel. I was starting to feel uncomfortable as she rushed in from the streets and practically sat down with no preparation, no cleansing and no ritual before she started the reading. She was clever, though; she must have sensed my uneasiness as she quickly went in to find out what I desired the most. I was surprised at how hasty I was to offer her information without even realising I was doing so. I mean, come on, I'm a professional psychic myself! I do have a few of the old tricks up my sleeve too when you are struggling to tap into a client, but this was more than a trick. This was sensationalism and acting at its finest, and I fell hook, line and sinker. By the end of the session, I found myself heading over to the nearest ATM to hand over to Dalia $500US in order to make sure the evil curses and hexes placed on me (both of which I don't believe in anyway) would come nowhere near myself or my family. It was almost like I was in a trance-like state, and robotically, I followed her lead as she walked me straight to the teller machine herself.

Later that night, in our hotel room overlooking some of the steepest San Francisco roads I had ever seen, I wondered how on earth did I fall for the oldest trick in the book when it comes to fortune-tellers. Still, I held hope that she was indeed praying and meditating and removing whatever malevolent demon was within me, considering the special candles she needed from Israel, that were to be covered in sacred oils, and blessed by some of the Highest, were truly worth the $500 I had just handed over.

A few days later, just as we finished walking the famous winding and ever-turning Lombard Street, I received a phone call from Dalia. It seemed fitting that a crooked psychic was to ring as I was walking the crooked street. Her voice was panicky, and she frantically needed to buy more blessed candles as the curse put upon me by some ancient master in lifetimes gone by was too strong for the ritual she had completed for me the night before. She needed to do more, and this time she needed to upgrade her candles. $4000 worth of candles, to be exact! As she explained how Satan had impregnated my mother and I was indeed his child, the urgency in her voice deserved an Oscar-winning accolade, and she may have even fooled me if I had not known better. And in true Colin form, he started to call me from Sydney just to check in and see how our holiday was going. All the while, Dalia was going on and on about hexes and curses. After the impeccable timing of Colin's call, I then relayed Dalia's message back to Ross. He laughed and shook his head and took full credit that he is the one who always has to pull me away from "that shit," as he likes to call it. Taking the advice from the mother in "My Big Fat Greek Wedding," I let Ross think he was right because, the truth is, there was no way I was ever going to fall for that shit anyway. Well, no more than I already had.

A few days later, contemplating how Dalia can sleep at night, I called her to let her know how I felt about her scheming little business and how ashamed she should be of herself. As we were boarding our flight to New York, I received a message from Dalia wishing me the curse of a thousand years, and as I read her vile words, I smiled and knew that one day she too would be in the book I was going to write. And just for the record, I secretly did say my prayers before our plane flew off…just in case!

Chapter 5

Namaste

"Before you judge someone, walk a mile in their shoes."

Not only does every new client come from a different background, but they all have their own unique stories and concerns. Each client has different aspirations, dreams, and hopes, but in the end, they all want just one thing – to be happy.

As a psychic, this does make matters a bit tricky because I have to be very careful not to discriminate between my clients. From very rich to very poor, socialites, famous celebrities, and the average normal you and me folk, I have never treated one different from the other. I know, though, that my readings are much softer than other readers. I don't just say it like it is, and instead, I will beat around the bush in order to get the message across to my client in as gentle a manner as possible to make sure their feelings or their life as they know it feels valued and heard. I know a lot of other psychics don't agree with this style of reading, but seeing the distress in a client's eyes and the hope of hearing something they so badly want makes me weak at my knees, and I can't handle being the bearer of bad news.

Don't get me wrong. I don't lie either, I just have this knack of telling the truth to the client even if it is not what they want to hear, but I know how to do it softly, gently and with compassion. That has always been one of my strengths, and the harder a client is, the more I seem to break through with them. There is nothing I love more than going to bed at night thinking how tough a customer was when she walked in and how soft she walked out, with a smile on her face to add.

It gives me great pleasure to hear various people's backgrounds and stories. That said, I make sure not to ask too many questions, as I think it is best to respect their privacy and give them peace of mind which then allows them to tell me everything themselves once they feel comfortable. One big misconception about psychics is that we are so good we actually know the client's name before they sit down, what they ate for breakfast that morning, and most importantly, what colour underwear they are wearing that day. Let me be the first to say it doesn't work that way, and if it did, then you will definitely be seeing headlines in the papers about psychics winning the lottery and cashing up big at the races. My brother is the best example of this as after 50 years of knowing me, he still thinks that a psychic must automatically know everything about you. Whenever I call him to ask a question, whether it be about a date of a family dinner or how the kids are, he will always smile and very cheekily say to me, "You are the psychic, you tell me?"Arghhhhh…brothers, they just don't get any better as they get older!

There have been times when I just could not read for someone. It happens, and when it does, I have to be honest enough to say to that client that I just can't seem to get through. Maybe I am having a bad day, or maybe they are so closed that not even the world's toughest truck could get through the thick armour they are wearing and using to hide the world from the pain they are really in.

Our number one policy at Embrace is that if one of our psychics is having trouble with a reading, we tell the client the truth and either offer them their money back immediately or ask if they would like to try another reader. Just as we all don't get along at times, it only makes sense that a psychic and a client don't always necessarily get along either, and their energies just don't gel.

There is another big misconception out there that a psychic can read you no matter where they are and at all times. I have never been a mind reader, except on occasions where my husband gets that look in his eyes, and I know exactly what he is thinking. In all seriousness, though, I don't just go out to the supermarket and start reading people as I am waiting in line to be served. For me, there is always a process of opening myself up and putting up my shield, as Colin likes to call it. "Put your shield up," he would always say as if the Trojan horse was just about to come into town.

If I need to close myself off, so I don't see, I can do that, and just as quickly, I can open myself so that I can see. It took me a lot of years to excel in this, but it has served its purpose on many occasions, especially when I have been out in crowds. I really don't want or need to know who is sleeping with who, or have somebody's long-lost Aunt Betty pester me as to where she really did hide the family jewels.

In my thirty years of professionally reading people, I have found that not all men are liars and cheaters and that a lot of women absolutely have a lot more to answer for. It was sometime in the late '90s when I came to this conclusion that more women out there were having affairs than men. I put it down that perhaps this is because more women come to me for readings than men, but as the years rolled on and plenty more men were open to psychic readings, my conclusion just didn't change.

Look, let's face it, more women will be most likely to be reading this book than men, and as a species, we have to admit that we are not only stronger than our male counterparts, we are just that touch smarter too, so women just don't seem to get themselves caught out. In other words, we are just that little bit sneakier.

A beautiful man with the eyes of a puppy dog would come to visit me for readings. As he sat in front of me with his eyes full of tears, I could feel his heartache, and I knew he was innocent. You see, his wife would frequent another psychic, someone who I had not known, and she had her convinced that Danny was molesting his children. The psychic also had her convinced that for an extra $600 a week, she could get rid of the evil curse on her children, and if she added an extra $250 a week, she would call on the incarnation of the Egyptian goddess, Isis, to give her that extra protection. Many years went by, and I bumped into Danny, he had all his children with him, and his now ex-wife had gone bankrupt as she could no longer afford her psychic's fees. The children were now at the age to decide that they wanted to live with their father, and I smiled because I knew that this man was innocent all along.

You will find a lot of psychics who like to ask questions and then tell their clients the things that they read between the lines, or they use body language as a dead giveaway as to what is going on for their clients. As much as I take my work very seriously, I will be the first to admit that there have been times when I just couldn't help but read the fidgets or the expressions on my clients' faces or the way they are dressed and present themselves. If any psychic tells you that they don't do this, then don't believe them because they absolutely do, even if they have no idea they are.

However, one thing I can be certain about is that no matter who the client is, at the end of the day, they all want the same thing – to be loved, to find happiness, and to feel acknowledged. I have never discriminated yet, and as I break down the years of clients, their ultimate goal is always the same, even if the stories and faces are completely different.

And as Lin Manuel Miranda once said, "Love doesn't discriminate between the sinners and the saints."

I don't think there is anything I haven't heard. When I first started, I was in my twenties and still very young. I was a good psychic, but I had absolutely no life skills and was totally naïve about the rest of the world. I was definitely not streetwise, and so to come across stories that, to me, came out of Hollywood, I quickly learned that there were some very sad stories out there, some really crazy people, and some pretty scary characters. If it were not for my Friday night circles with Janine and the girls, I am not sure what else could have got me through some of the narratives I sat through. I cried with my clients, laughed with them, made jokes, and we compared stories, but most of all, I noticed a common thread that even though I was the psychic and I should have done most of the talking, most of the clients just wanted to be heard. I have also found that the majority of the time, these people already know the answers deep inside themselves, but they are desperate for someone else to confirm it for them.

I will never forget Mindy, who walked into my reading room, and instantly I knew she was scared to say what she had to tell me. She fidgeted, she slurred her words, and she had fear in her eyes. My first thought was that someone, perhaps her husband, was being abusive towards her, and she was reaching out for help. I thought I knew exactly what was going on, and as soon as I did a spread of the cards, I felt nauseous. Her very own father had been having his own little fun with her five-year-old son, and I felt sick. In fact, I wanted to vomit, and I did just that as soon as she had left my room. I had no idea how to break it to her, but she did the hard job for me and broke it to me instead, and all she really wanted was for me to confirm what she already knew. Because it was such a sensitive subject, I refused to say anything except refund her money. I insisted that she went straight to the police. I made it clear that if she didn't, I would, as I had a duty of care to that innocent little child. I must admit that even though an open mind and being non-judgemental has to come with the territory of being psychic, I quickly realised that I was extremely judgemental, and not enough of any open minds could have swayed me otherwise when it came to men like this.

Another one of my clients was a beautiful young girl who would always come dressed up in Armani or Louis

Vuitton, carrying an expensive matching handbag, wearing exquisite heels, and completed her look with an amazing hairstyle every time I saw her. She was really pretty, and her nails were always immaculate. Anyone would have immediately thought she had been born into money when this statement was further from the truth than possible. I will always remember her pretty face but cannot remember her name. When she was quite young, this girl's mother walked out on her and her father, leaving a five-year-old miss to fend for herself as her dad was a severe alcoholic. Over the years, she had no choice but to grow up way too quickly than her age, and as she hit eighteen, her father became terminally ill with liver cancer.

Becoming the sole caregiver of her father, she went into survival mode and sold her body for a decent amount of moolah. Obviously, her father never found out her secret, but I think he was way too sick to even question or bother to know where the money for his medicines was coming from. Although she didn't like what she was doing, she had become addicted to the money, and yet, in each and every one of our sessions, all she ever wanted to know is if she would one day find her prince charming.

I hope she did, but from what I could see and from where I sat, the future didn't look too bright, and just like I predicted, she stopped coming for readings after I had found out she had been severely bashed to the point of non-recognition by a deranged jealous client. I think about her often and pray she got out of the cycle, but it was so long ago that she is either still playing the game or lying next to her father, who eventually passed away.

I don't know if whatever I had to say to her actually helped or gave her any hope for the future, but I do know for certain that I gave her acceptance, and that can be a very healing experience to someone who couldn't even accept themselves.

If you like to hear the neighbourhood gossip and keep in the loop, then I recommend doing what I do for a living as it is the very next step towards being a fly on the wall in most people's homes. In fact, we absolutely know more than hairdressers, and our secrets are much juicier! There were times when I busted at my seams to not give away any secrets of the locals, but I had always kept my composure and integrity about me even when the news was as juicy as a ripe piece of fruit. In this instance, it was someone close to home and a well-known psychic healer in our community. Damn, I really had to keep my mouth shut on this one, but like the Cheshire cat, I couldn't keep that cheeky grin off my face.

Marcella, a mother of two and married to a workaholic, was having an affair with a so-called healer who was apparently well and truly healing the socks off her. Mark was an odd-looking man but carried a composure of confidence and awe that made him attractive to vulnerable women who really needed some love in their lives. According to Marcella, Mark had convinced her that they were soul mates, and while she was asleep, he would come to her at the witching hour via astral travel and made mad, deep, passionate love to her while her husband, who lay by her side, snored his previous day away.

I felt bad for Marcella because I totally felt the urgency in her voice as she questioned me as to when Mark would leave his wife for her. I have to tell you, I totally got baffled myself when straight after Marcella left the reading, in walked Cindy. Cindy, a psychic herself, sat down and practically repeated Marcella's story word for word. As confusion started to set into my ever-weary mind that day, I certainly woke myself up when Cindy mentioned the name, Mark. I was like, WTF! Except those abbreviations were not around in those days, so I'm pretty sure I was thinking a whole lot more.

As the weeks went on, more and more Marcellas and Cindys walked in, all with different names, different faces, all worked in the psychic industry, and yet, all believed that Mark was their true soul mate. Obviously, this was something I could not tell anyone as the women who trusted me truly believed they were each Mark's one and only. It got a bit tricky when, at a psychic fair, I bumped into almost all of Mark's lovers under the same roof. I smiled, and in order to protect their privacy and their secrets, I kept walking on.

To this day, whenever I hear Mark's name pop up in conversation, I cringe as he is still many years on playing the same game, some of the same women plus a whole lot more. You see, it becomes dangerous when men use this industry as a means to get sex and abuse their power of trust with these susceptible women. Usually, I find it happens as a means of "healing," then comes the massages in order to tense their weary muscles and then come the happy endings with lots of $$$s, cash in hand, thank you very much,

Ma'am, and all in the name of healing and unconditional love.

You just have to take a look at the likes of John of God, who will now spend the rest of his days locked up behind a prison wall. The saddest thing about this is that I have come across many Marks and Johns of God in this industry, and over the years, the abuse and misuse of trust astounds me; how can these men get away with it? Sleazy is the only word that I can come up with when I think about these schemers.

Take Paulie, for example, a pretty young blonde who popped into Embrace late one Saturday afternoon. Her shorts were way too short, and she was wearing a gorgeous white tweed shirt that shouted out femininity at its finest. Her dilemma was that she needed something, perhaps a crystal, to help her orgasm, as in all her twenty-eight years on this planet, this was something she just couldn't bring herself to do. We had a chat, I suggested a few crystals and relaxation methods, and two weeks later, she practically danced right up to my counter and shouted through the rooftops. Something had definitely changed for her; she was ecstatic and oozed sex appeal to the extent that if I hadn't known her story, I could have sworn she had been having orgasms all week long.

I asked if I could have some of whatever it was she was having, and she directed me to a healer she had met online, who was now helping her with her climaxing problem. I sort of thought for a moment before that that maybe I had stumbled upon some secret stone that could make me a fortune and have women all over the world shining bright the way Paulie was that day in my store. The suggested crystal definitely met its match with the male gigolo. Oops, I meant to say healer! I now rest my case.

I have so many stories, I could probably write ten books just on the clients and customers I have had the pleasure of meeting every day at Embrace. They trust me with their lives and their money, and I will be forever grateful for their patronage, dramas, adventures, and never-ending stories. The number of times I have wiped tears away from another goddess's face or laughed until our tears ran down our legs, I have come to understand the true meaning of the words I so often hear in my work "Namaste" – The light in me sees the light in you.

Even when unable to help someone, a genuine psychic would take out the time to advise her clients well instead of insisting they come back over and over for yet another reading. I understand that many people prefer to see a psychic in replacement for a councillor, but when that psychic has had no formal training or has not got their own shit together, then it really becomes a game of Russian roulette. Any respectable psychic will refer their client to a professional or even to another psychic for another opinion.

I have had eighteen-year-old girls wanting desperately to know when their forty-three-year-old lovers were going to leave their wives and kids, eighty-year-old women asking when they would find love, mothers wanting to know if their children are OK, and business people trusting me with decisions on their billions of investment dollars. Celebrities, politicians, doctors, lawyers, judges, university lecturers, mafia, grandmothers, mums and dads, retail workers, criminals, junkies, strippers, sex workers, midwives, young teenagers, sports stars, movie stars, tradies, and office workers, you name it I have read for them, including people who couldn't even speak English!

A funny memory; I was doing a reading for a young man who had the whole 'full of himself' attitude but had the looks to go with it and a body of a bulldog. I actually remember telling him that he reminded me of a bulldog, and that is when he asked if I knew who he was. Baffled and convinced I had never seen his face before, I went on to tell him that I saw fame, girls and lots of them, and money all around him. He wasn't giving me any help and sat with his arms tightly crossed around his chest, which meant that I was really struggling to get through to him and actually read him properly. I felt like the reading was a complete flop until I heard his friend ask, "How was it?" as they were leaving the store. "She knew who I was," he said, which automatically put me into detective mode to find out who he actually was. Looking his name up in the diary, I Googled his name, and there he was, a famous football player for Canterbury bulldogs, a well-known rugby league football team here in Australia. Bingo! I had nailed his reading even when I thought I had just flopped.

People have an uncanny way of giving me a glimpse into their lives and yet portray a completely different life to those around them. Take Sinead, for example. She was a high-powered career woman who made loads of money at the stock exchange. She was always well presented, yet there was a shyness about her that gave her a touch of mystery. She was easy to read, and I got to see the rawness behind the glamour of her corporate world. She came across as a high-powered career woman whose petite face I will never forget, but it was the opposite when she got between the sheets at night. Her husband, who she so badly was in love with, insisted she sleep with other men while he sat back and enjoyed the show. She told me how much she hated doing it, but she always wanted to please her husband. I was a little taken aback at first, but now I never look at things or people as they seem on the outside. Everyone has their story, their cross to bear, along with a few skeletons in the cupboard.

Poor Catherine. She was definitely a character and a half and someone who, by looking at her, seemed quite normal in the normal sense of the word. She called Embrace one raining Sunday afternoon wanting to know why her boyfriend did not want to come back to her. As Catherine was a little special and we knew her well, I was able to tell her that I didn't have time to talk that day as we were super busy, and perhaps we could talk later that day. I had heard this story a million times over, and she and I always went in circles, never really getting anywhere with it.

Later that afternoon, when I took a trip to the bathroom, I walked back into Embrace to find Ross entertaining Catherine on the phone. His words, "Well, that would do it," were enough for my ears to perk up and ask what was going on. There was one fine detail Catherine had been forgetting to tell me about her boyfriend, and that was that she was sleeping with her boyfriend's brother. In a matter of 5 minutes, Ross, who is not a psychic, I may add, was able to extract this bit of information out of her more than the three months I had been talking to her.

Another customer came in with her daughter wanting to book a reading with a psychic as she had lost her cat that morning and wanted to know where it was. I will never forget Ross piping in, asking if they had looked up in the large tree that was rooted firmly in the customer's backyard, and with that, they left the shop to do so. In a normal business environment, you wouldn't want to miss a sale, but we just couldn't bring ourselves to take money from the woman until she had exhausted all her avenues. And besides, it was going to take more than a fortune teller to let her know where her cat had gone. Sure enough, later that afternoon, the lady called Embrace and asked to speak to Psychic Ross to thank him for his advice, as her ginger-haired, much-loved cat was most definitely taking residence in the big eucalyptus tree out in the back. At times, it just takes a bit of common sense and not a psychic to help you get back on track.

One of my scariest encounters was with Vlado. He had come straight from a court hearing and wanted to know if he would be sent on the next plane back to Serbia for crimes he had committed. Just sitting near him, I knew they were serious crimes. He scared me and made me very nervous. I could smell death on him, and his eyes had no soul. He knew that his presence was making me uncomfortable, and he also knew that I could see something I did not want to say. He became agitated and insisted I tell him what I could see. It didn't help the matter that I started to cry because his energy was way too much for me, and it was making me feel sick. He wasn't a very nice man, and I asked him to leave.

A week later, I received a phone call from Phillipa. She got my number from a friend of a friend and asked if I could attend her home with a bunch of girlfriends for a group reading. The money was good, the event sounded fun, and I was single and had nothing planned for my Friday night, so I couldn't see why not. She opened the apartment door with a big Alsatian by her side. I am a huge dog lover, but there was something about this dog that made me feel uncomfortable. I then noticed that there was no group of women and after I had entered and Phillipa closed the door behind me, in walked Vlado from another room. I wanted to vomit. I shook, and I froze, and I knew I had to get out of there. Instead, Phillipa got out of there as she closed the door behind her and yelled out, "Enjoy your reading!"

Vlado went on to explain how he needed me back to tell him what I had seen, and I knew that I had seen too much and that maybe I too would end up where some of his unfortunate victims had taken their final rest. He was calmer than the first time I met him, and he assured me he meant no harm. I think he could smell my sweat, and he was definitely no stranger to fear, especially from his victims. I knew I had nowhere else to go, so I got my trusty cards out, and I read him.

I told him about the crimes back in Serbia, and then I lied. If he was to be deported, he was going to face an execution squad, and that is all he wanted to know. Was he going to be sent back to his country? I told him that he will be safe here in Australia, and they will not deport him and that he would live happily ever after amongst our Australian folk. He was happy with that.

I then told Vlado that I had to leave as my 'boyfriend' (the boyfriend I didn't have) was waiting for me at home. It was with that he banged his large hand down on the table, my cards flew to the floor, and he told me that I wasn't going anywhere until I ate some of the cake he had made for me. This time I was convinced it had been laced with poison and that after eating it, I would wake up in a container cell with other young women and being sold off to some eastern bloc country, never to be seen again.

I then told him I was on a diet and allergic to eggs, or flour, or chocolate. I can't remember which, but he knew I was a bad liar, and he made me eat it. That big horrible dog was standing there watching me, and I started to say my prayers.

I don't even remember how I got out of there that night, and I definitely have no memory of how I got home, but in the end, Vlado, too, just wanted some company and to hear a glimmer of hope even though his crimes against humanity didn't deserve any. I never saw or heard from Vlado again after that, but I knew his fate was only a few weeks in front of that chilling Friday night as soon as he had boarded his plane.

I learnt very quickly to become non-judgemental once I was in that back room, and I learnt how to deal with and approach all different types of personality traits. Some needed the cold hard truth, some needed to be pussy-footed around, and some just wanted to talk while I said hardly anything. I also learnt that we all have our individual lessons to learn in this lifetime and that I had no right to judge another soul fulfiling their karma. It is not always an easy thing, especially when something does not sit right with you.

I will be forever grateful to these clients who, in turn, helped me become a much more understanding and tolerant person, and it was they who helped my heart remain soft.

We have discussed some of the clients in this chapter, would you like to know about some of the fake psychics? Let's discuss them in Chapter 7, shall we?

Chapter 6

Are You the One?

"Ego is a dress for insecurity."

I will never forget Sylvie. As I entered her home for the very first time, she embraced me with a hug that I felt would crush my delicate frame, and I remember my sunglasses that were perched on my head falling to the floor. She was like the big mamma bear, and instantly I knew that I was in the right hands, or should I say arms?

She led me to her kitchen table, and there sat two other women, who were just as keen as I to learn metaphysics and paranormal phenomena. Just because I was psychic by nature did not give me exclusive access to the all-knowing eye of this world, as the terrain is so huge, and I had a burning desire to just want to know it all. It was here in Sylvie's kitchen that I learned the art of tarot, numerology, and astrology. Of course, everybody thinks their teacher is the best, and I was no exception. With a very heavy French accent as she was taught by the gypsies back in France, Sylvie taught me how to read the cards. They came second nature to me, and yet, to this day, I still find myself reading them, but not really reading them. Only another psychic will understand what I mean by this, but the cards were merely used as a tool; my real talent lay in what I already knew how to do, and that was channelling and seeing.

Over the four years I worked with Sylvie, I dabbled a little in numerology and astrology. As mathematics was never my strong subject, I found astrology too hard with all the charts and mathematical degrees. As I worked with somebody's numbers, I was constantly using my fingers to add them up. Don't get me wrong, I still use these modalities all these years later, but not to the degree I work with the tarot and clairvoyance.

And so, my adventures in paranormal psychology with my very first teacher Sylvie began. What was meant to be a one-year gig turned into four years of learning everything I didn't know and polishing everything I did know. As I opened the pages to my exercise book to write down Sylvie's notes, her words became entrenched into my veins for the rest of my career in the spiritual world. In fact, just in my world in general.

Before she began, Sylvie told the class to write down the three Ds of spirituality. Number 1 – DUMP THE EGO! Number 2 – Dump Deduction and Number 3 – I actually don't remember! (Sorry, Sylvie).

DUMP THE EGO was the first thing etched into my psyche, and I found myself repeating those words over the years to staff, students, and readers who came to work with me at Embrace. Even my children at times, where I established with them from the beginning that being humble was much nobler than self-admiration.

My first lesson with Sylvie was all about the ego, and how many people try to become "famous" in the psychic world or believe they have a gift that is superior to everybody else. Sylvie told the class that this is further from the truth and if we were to work with ego, not only will Spirit eventually take our talent away, we would never really be authentic in our work. One thing that clearly stood out for me was the karma we would generate for ourselves if we abused this work.

I never missed a class with Sylvie, and even though I don't remember some of the modules and I wasn't interested in some of the others, I totally immersed myself in her wise words, and the whole ego thing stood out to me the most. This was back in the day before the internet, and we had no Google to find ourselves a million and one psychics, especially the ones who just woke up one day, and all of a sudden, they were psychics. If it were that easy, I am still waiting to wake up to find myself singing my lungs away and finally taking that well dreamt of a bow on the stage. Coming to think of it, my classes were long before GPS, and I clearly remember trying to read the street map as I drove, book in hand as I turned pages to drive an hour each Monday night to Sylvie's. How times have changed.

Born in Paris, Sylvie came from a long line of gypsies who read cards and fortunes as a living. Her ancestors read for royalty and aristocrats, and Sylvie's childhood was spent learning the family traditions from her grandmother. At 14, Sylvie was being paid to read for clients. I feel blessed that I met this woman as I felt my classes were really lessons in self-development, and I grew to become very confident in myself and my work.

Everybody has an ego. I have an ego. You have an ego. Ego gives us a process to identify ourselves to others yet can become dangerous when used against others to show any type of superiority or 'better than' mentality. From my many years of working in the spiritual industry, I have seen ego come and go. I have seen people work it to their advantage, whilst others made fools of themselves, and those who were the real deal remained quiet and humble. Yet, modest people need to make money too. It is just a very different style to their show-off wannabe counterparts.

Quite a few years back, a national radio program came out in which a group of psychics all challenged themselves in situations to find out who was the country's most gifted psychic. At first, I thought it would be fun to listen to, as I personally knew quite a few of the psychics involved. Embrace was also excited that one of our resident readers had been selected for the show, and we proudly showed her off on all our social media channels and even had our customers involved in all the marketing.

Gina was a very quiet and timid reader in her pre-radio days. Always with a smile on her face, she came into work, did her job, and went home. We never heard a peep from her, no complaints, and she gave us no trouble. Actually, we liked the fact that Gina had a whole heap of medical accolades behind her name and that she was trained in psychology, life coaching, counselling, and personal development. It made us feel much more comfortable referring troubled clients to her, as we knew with her background, she had the know-how to deal with distraught personality types.

Personally, I didn't feel that Gina had psychic ability, and so we would always sell her readings as life coaching and/or counselling as this truly was her main qualification. Gina became known as our "intuitive" psychic, which meant that the information she received came from her own intuition, nothing else.

One week after the program aired, Gina came waltzing into Embrace with a whole new look about her and a completely different persona. It was like the old Gina was taken by aliens, and a clone had stepped into her body, replaced by a loud, obnoxious, attention-grabbing egomaniac. She placed her bag in the room and came marching out into the front of the store, erecting a big, and I mean BIG enormous, gigantic, massive banner with her face plastered all over it. At no time was I asked if this would be OK, especially because our shopping centre has strict rules on banners and the likes in their centre.

Gina then went on to explain that now that she is a national star (ummmm, the show was a short series, and she really didn't play the main role), she needed to have her banner in the front of the store. We all needed to practically bow down to her each and every demand, and she insisted that she be paid a hefty wage, as she was not like all our other "corner shop" readers. As soon as those words came out of her mouth, my antennas went up, and I had to bite my tongue so hard that it actually started to bleed.

I have always been about straightening another woman's crown when it is crooked, but this was taking the cake, and I was not having anyone whatsoever put another down in my store. My "corner shop" readers were much older, they didn't do social media, and in fact, as far as I was concerned, they were the real deal. Helen was one of them, and low and behold, anyone who would put my fairy godmother and adopted grandmother down. There was no prancing around or showing off amongst these corner shop readers, and we all came into work with our own gifts and combined them to create an atmosphere of total and utter pure love. I turned into a big mother hen, and I instantly became very protective about my other readers. It went against my very own grain of salt to have any preferences as far as favourites were concerned, and it was a very clear rule at Embrace that every psychic will be paid the same fee no matter what.

Lucky for us, Westfield security came along and told us that the banner had to go. It was an occupational health and safety issue, so that took some pressure off us girls when we had to face this narcissistic, borderline personality woman. What came next is what surprised me most. Remember I told you that Gina was a life coach? She taught and helped people pretty much how to get their shit together, and it was at this moment that I realized Gina was nowhere near having any of her life in order. I knew Gina was not happy at Embrace, she didn't fit the mould, and nobody was bowing down to her. When she called me into her reading room to have a "chat," which really translated into her making demands that were far beyond reasonable, I instantly knew I was working with a loose cannon.

Once again, Celina became a target and somehow got into Gina's firing line. Not only being one of my dearest and closest friends, Celina was also the manager of Embrace. With her long blonde curls, amazingly ocean blue eyes, Celina is the epitome of beauty inside and out. It was not uncommon for casting agents to run up to her in restaurants and cafes and hand out their business cards. It also wasn't uncommon for some of the funniest men I can think of, to hang around Embrace like dogs on heat in the hope that Celina would find a glimmer of attractiveness in them. We all wanted to be closer to Celina. She just had that personality that oozed fun, beauty, freedom, and even more fun.

Celina's rostered days off were boring days indeed. An integral part of the shop, she had a knack for calming me down when I had to deal with crazy people, and in particular, people that I would call "nutters," who just had no concept of life at all. It took a lot to get me to the point of no return, but on this particular Wednesday morning, I was well and truly there, way before the lunchtime bell was about to ring.

As a boss, there comes a time when you need to make a crucial decision for the sake of the business, and this day was no different. Gina sat me down and went for the kill. The venom that spat out of her mouth was worse than any poisonous scorpion sting, and I was horrified. Gina insisted that I fire Celina because she didn't like her husband talking to her when he came to pick Gina up from work. As Gina's face turned greener and greener with envy, and her appalling words filled with hatred towards an innocent person, froth came spewing from her mouth, and I knew then and there that I had to fire Gina. As Gina, in all her fury, kept speaking and making herself look more and more foolish, I heard the words come straight out of my mouth, "You know what, Gina... you're fired!"

And just like that, Gina no longer worked at Embrace, and I walked out of that room, gave Celina a massive hug, cried a little on her shoulder, and whispered softly, "I'll tell you later." I am pretty sure Gina's ego got a little deflated that day, and I never did tell Celina later what was said behind those walls. I guess she will know now once she reads this book.

To be honest, we all felt a sigh of relief once Gina was out, it felt energetically lighter in the store, and everyone didn't seem to be working on eggshells anymore. We politely told clients that Gina had left Embrace to pursue her own career and left it at that, until one day, not even two weeks after Gina had left, phone calls started to come into the shop. A woman on the other end of the line was quite distressed and explained to me how she had a reading with

Gina at our store a few months prior, and Gina took it upon herself to 'gossip' about the reading to other psychics. This poor woman felt betrayed, and I didn't blame her. I mean, it comes with the territory that everything said in the back room is said in utmost confidence, and a client's personal story remains sacred between them and their reader. We all know that whatever happens in Vegas stays in Vegas well, the same is true with a psychic reading. Whatever happens in that back room stays in that back room!

Sadly, I knew this woman was telling me the truth as Gina had told us all about a reading she had done with a prominent footballer's wife. Their marriage was on the rocks, and she suspected her husband had not only been cheating on her, but he had also been hiding money in an offshore account that she did not know anything about. Not only did I know this woman personally, I knew she would be horrified if she knew that I knew the secrets she was keeping. Gina couldn't help but come straight out of that reading and tell the staff everything, from the affair to the money, to the fact that this woman was also hiding a very serious illness that no one was to know about. I had to remind Gina that it was not for us to know and cut the conversation short, as I quickly reminded her about the unspoken word of ethics and professionalism. So, it became no surprise when Gina's client telephoned to tell me that the whole of the Sutherland Shire now knew her story and how disappointed she was in not only Gina but in Embrace itself. I was left to apologise profusely as there was not much more I could do. I felt shame that we were fooled by Gina, that she truly believed in the diva she had become, and that the innocent clients had been betrayed by her trust.

A lot was said about me after Gina left Embrace, and once again, I had my conscience and Celina hold me together when Gina's lies became the talk of the 'psychic' community which I had known. It was very hard to let it go and not defend myself, but as time moved along, the rumours started to diminish along with Gina's reputation and career.

A year after we fired Gina, Gina's husband walked into the shop crying and needing a psychic reading. I took him into the backroom, with his tears still wet on my shoulder, and just had a chat with him instead. Gina had left him with their four children and ran off with another married man who promised her fame and fortune. Gina had no other choice than to reinvent herself and started a kindness project that consisted of life coaching and whatever else she could fool herself into believing she was.

I've come across a few Ginas in my career who preach one thing but practice another. Don't get me wrong, we are all guilty at times of doing the same, as I am forever telling my children to clean up after themselves, to find that I am actually the only messy one in our household. Needless to say, there is a difference between hurting another in doing so because of a superiority complex or doing so just because you can.

Very early on, when I had just started in the industry, there was no Facebook, Instagram, or any social media whatsoever. The internet was still quite new, so it was impossible to know everyone who was working in the industry unless you knew them personally. In 2005 when I became pregnant with my twins, I decided to stop reading professionally in order to protect my unborn babies from the different energies and stories that would soak into my psyche. I became very protective of my personal space, and it was here that I realized how much crap we actually can take on as a psychic reader. All of a sudden, I became much lighter and happier as I only had me and my half-cooked twins to worry about. A good psychic, however, knows how to keep themselves heavily protected around the energies their clients can bring. I always felt safe and guarded, and I never left my home for the day without my protection, prayers, and barriers going up. It didn't mean I didn't care for my clients; in fact, it was the opposite as I found that I was caring too much. As an empath, it was hard not to take on their emotions, and so once the decision was made to become a housewife for a while, I came back to the industry with a whole new ball game.

All of a sudden, a click on Google would give me millions (slight exaggeration) of psychic sites. No longer would magazines and newspapers hold ads for pay-by-the-minute ring a psychic. Instead, they were plastered all over social media, and either I was very naïve and was kept under a rock, but all of a sudden, everyone and anyone was a psychic. There were people I had never heard of who suddenly woke up one day, and they had "powers." Good old fair dinkum Aussie men who held a beer in one hand and the remote control to the sports channel in the other, managed to tap into the secrets of the ancients and all of a sudden found themselves becoming shamans.

Women who married young and spent their vital

years as mothers and housewives suddenly needing a purpose in their lives when the kids moved out became mediums and high priestesses, and almost every second person was a Reiki master and healer.

Psychics were glorified on television shows, and 'celebrity psychic' became the "in" word. I mean, if you weren't reading for movie stars and high-profile personalities, you just were not good at your game. Everyone needed a "Seen on TV" logo on their business cards and banners, and well-known festivals and events became infested with mystic seers who had the secret to the Universe that you and I weren't told about. Even I missed out on the undisclosed information that only the true lightworkers were apparently given, and just like that, my work, my sacred cherished industry, and my divine knowledge became a big fat joke.

I found morals and ethics to be a thing of the past, whilst the backstabbers and fame whores took all the attention. Being on the stage was only for the very best, but my question remained as to who made them the very best? Was it that they knew how to market themselves well on social media and had money to back themselves up with paid 'likes' and false followers? Why was this person in a photo with that person when this person was talking about that person in a derogatory fashion just the day before? How did this person become a love guru when I knew them personally, and for years had to listen to them first-hand recall over and over again how they can't find love? Psychics who couldn't find a relationship no matter how much Feng Shui they did around their love corner became worshipped as experts on finding love. Then there were the financial psychic experts who can help you with your business when they have never had a business of their own. They came to work eating vegemite sandwiches because they couldn't afford to buy themselves lunch, let alone a takeaway $2.00 cup of coffee or tea! These were the very same psychics who asked me for an advance on their pay each and every week.

I have seen it all, and inevitably, I have had to work with them all too. I questioned over and over as the years rolled on how a manager of a takeaway lunch restaurant all of a sudden became a shaman. Not any old shaman either, mind you, I'm talking about an international healer, who brought so much of his personal shit to work, and as the crap came out of his mouth, I would always remember Colin's face, shaking his head like he just heard a really bad joke, and reciting his favourite Batman words "Holy Moly!"

Then there were "healers" that couldn't come to work because they were always sick. In fact, they were sick more times than they actually did come to work. Maybe because they smoked like chimneys all day and constantly ate junk food, yet they somehow had the magic touch to help everybody heal except themselves.

One of my all-time favourites was a Reiki master who worked with energy and could not bear to be placed in a room with someone she deemed had bad energy. Apparently, it would give her a headache, and her vibration was so high that a person with a low vibration could make her quite ill, and therefore, she would need to then take days off to heal herself better. What made it all the funnier (or really sadder) was that we had endless complaints about how rude she was to customers, and people did not like walking into the shop because her energy was so bad and her manner so rude. I only needed to take one look at the friends she hung out with to know that she had to go. Reiki practitioners are a dime a dozen, and no matter how high up the scale they are or what amazing teaching facilities they train, they too can have a nice lucrative home-based business. Their work is based on an energy that can keep the taxman at bay and lead the gullible, high-paying clients to a never-ending money pit because their energy is as bad as their clients.

Please don't get me wrong here, as I also know many Reiki masters and healers who are more than amazing, and I am not in any way saying that all Reiki healers are bad news.

I truly believe, and I say this because I have witnessed it personally, almost daily, over a 30-year period, that a lot of people turn to spirituality and psychic/healing work because they believe it gives them a sense of importance, an edge over others in order to say, "Hey look at me, I am better than you. I know something you don't know, I can hear something you can't hear, and God/the Universe loves me so much more than you as he chose ME to be his messenger!"

Yes, I know that this statement will create a huge uproar in the spiritual community, so let's just wait and see who will yell the loudest, shall we? The dark will always know our weaknesses, so it is important not to let it in.

Believe me when I say that just because somebody has a certificate in Reiki, or Tarot, or psychic readings, or any other modality that gives them a sense of importance over another, does not mean that they have tapped into a universal force that you have not. I, too, have received certificates for courses I have done over the years, but I can assure you that they do not mean a thing. I have a certificate in astrology, and I still cannot read a chart! I also have a certificate in hospitality and barrister training, but I have no idea how to make a decent cappuccino. And the best certificate I received was when I decided to give pole dancing a go, just for the exercise component, and yet I was the only one who couldn't stay up on that god-damn pole! I giggle ever so slightly as I recall sliding down the pole and spending most of my time on the floor. That certificate takes pride of place in my office as a reminder that a piece of paper can make you be whoever you want to be.

It is most definitely fun to learn as much as you can from other psychics and to see alternative ways that others may teach, but I can assure you that sitting down and saying your prayers, being grateful, creating a sacred space, and manifesting miracles through rituals does not require you to pay someone a shit load of money in order for a miracle or healing to occur. You don't need a certificate on the wall for that either!

To me, this is when you are giving your power away to a "healer" who was more than likely yelling hysterically at her kids only a few hours earlier, cursing because she is in a loveless marriage, and maliciously gossiping about another colleague before turning herself into a chameleon of love and light as you enter her door. Trust me. I worked with her, I know!

I truly hope that people can see all along the true power they have in themselves and that they do not need to search for heroes or demigods. This is the time to ponder the mighty words that Glinda, the good witch in The Wizard of Oz, gave to Dorothy…"You had the power all along, my dear, you just had to learn it for yourself."

So next time you want to give your power away, just remember it could be to someone who really needs their ego stroked, another notch on their belt, and another excuse to believe they are better than what they actually are.

Ego has a funny way of changing a person. Just when you think you know somebody, you realise you do not know them at all. I will never forget the first boss I worked for in this industry, we all looked up to her, and she portrayed this air of worldly elegance and mysticism. In a way, we all felt intimidated by her as we truly believed she was greater than thou, and her mission in this world was to make it a better place. I was young then; it was back in the days I believed in gurus and heroes when you believed what you were told and left it at that. Experience and time made me wise, and a soft heart made me pure, and as I threw away all the bad experiences and saved the lessons, I was drawn more and more each day to the people who have now become my tribe.

I found myself on the phone with Colin late into the evenings, distressed by how some of these people were still getting away with what I had considered atrocious behaviour. He lectured me on judgement and how I cannot change a person who didn't see an issue with their actions. That is when it hit me, and I knew then and there that I needed to be silent in order to be confident and strong. I didn't need to worry about another's behaviour; I just needed to worry about my own and what I had set out to achieve with Embrace.

I must admit I would always find myself chuckling when I would have a whine to Colin about another show-off, and he would always tell me that big egos have small ears, and he would always pull on my ears as he said it, in order to make mine grow just that little bit more. Just as it is difficult not to eat the last piece of hot apple pie, the same is true when it came to not paying attention to the egotist. Even though Colin didn't say it directly and left it so I could work it out on my own, I soon realised that my reaction to these people made me just as bad as them, as my ego was starting to feel deflated and belittled. Sylvie appeared time and time in my dreams with her strong romantic French accent "Dump the Ego," and as I learned to eat humble pie, I actually started liking its taste.

Tell me about one person who doesn't feel they need to justify themselves as to how good they are at the expense of another, and I will give you a million dollars! We have all been guilty, but it is in not realizing it and not doing something about it where the error lies.

A prominent American psychic came to visit Embrace and do some work with us. Ross and I bent over backwards to make her feel welcome, give her some good old Aussie hospitality and entertain her each night until she left to go back home. Staying at our home for a week, I cooked on a few occasions, but most of the time, we went out to eat, and of course, as the ethnic in both Ross and I would have it, we paid for everything. We didn't mind, we were happy to do it, but it was at the stroke of midnight when I couldn't keep my eyes open any longer. I couldn't listen to another piece of gossip from this ever-popular psychic. She bitched, and she did not stop bitching. Her stage appearances were angelic, but behind closed doors, I heard it all, and I knew each and everyone's dirty laundry along with how clear it was she did not like them, even though she had taken loads of photos with them earlier that day.

I knew it was only going to be a matter of time that she would talk about me, and of course, it came back to me as quick as a boomerang with wings. You see, apparently, this love and light person thought it was good that I was fatter than her and that I looked a lot older even though we were the same age. Honestly, I didn't even notice (until it had become apparent), but the way she got her rocks off on it was seriously a problem. In my eyes anyway. It was here when her ego got in the way of some really good work she was actually doing, and she became more consumed about her looks and appearance to the detriment of her friends.

People asked me if what she had said about me had bothered me, and the truth is it hadn't. I was bigger than her, and yes, she did have a youthful appearance, so that in itself was not the problem. What did, however, play on me a bit was that she felt the need to say it to other people. She couldn't be satisfied that she had a successful career, a wonderful husband and truly was very talented in her work. Her ego screamed out for more, and that therein is where the danger lies. Again, I hear Colin's words as I type this, that an envious friend is always a dangerous enemy.

I lost one of my best friends because of ego. In the end, they made it very clear that I was not good enough to hang around in their circle anymore, as I was not classified in their eyes as a celebrity. I had taught this person everything they needed to know, introduced them to the right connections, and had given them their head start in their career. I loved this person who became a huge part of my life, but I knew it was time to say goodbye when our conversations became all about them and how good they were. No longer stopping to ask how I was or how the kids were. I would sit hours upon hours to listen to how the paparazzi (which we don't even have here in Australia anyway) were following my friend and how people were noticing them everywhere they went. Unless the two of us were looking through two different lenses, I never noticed.

I do wonder about this person from time to time and hope that they realise their true worth within themselves without having to convince the whole world about it. You see, ego is one of the worst poisons in the world, and it is more lethal to our wellbeing than anything else. People have lost relationships and careers because of their inflated egos, and in the spiritual world, there is just absolutely no room for it.

Inner peace will never come to anyone when they work with ego, and in order to be at peace within ourselves, we must keep our ego for our bad hair days instead!

Chapter 7

The F Word – FAKE!

"Don't trust everything you see... Even salt looks like sugar"

- Deborah King

The way the world is headed today, we are in for some really deep shit. I fear for our children, our mental health, and Mother Earth's fury as we lose our power to find it again in a new romance, a new car, the latest fashion accessory, and even perhaps a psychic! Even better, an "As Seen on TV" psychic, and even better than that a "celebrity psychic," and even better than that an "As Seen on TV celebrity psychic" with certificates and lots of them and even much, much better than that, an As Seen on TV celebrity psychic with lots of certificates who suddenly woke up one day and became a psychic in their sleep! Bingo, the world is your oyster!

But what if everything we have ever known is a lie?

We already don't trust our governments, we can't believe everything we hear in the media, the girl next door is sleeping with the happily married man down the road, JFK Junior isn't really dead, and god forbid your psychic, the one who tells you everything you want to know, is a fake!

There comes a time in a person's life when they just can't sit back and watch any more injustice being done. Suddenly you find the inner strength inside you to do the right thing even though you know that you will be persecuted, made fun of, and thrown to the lions. I guess the time for me is now. Thirty years is a long time to watch fake psychic after fake psychic cash in the big bucks, take innocent, vulnerable people for a ride and make fun of something that I hold so sacred and dear. I can't change the world, but my words in this book may be able to change my little corner of the world.

Let me tell you a story about my old mate, Greg. A self-proclaimed Shaman who quit his job as a baker, woke up after a long night of drinking and, in some alcohol-infused abyss, heard the word of the Lord and became a psychic. I approached Greg one day as an old friend of mine had brought in a photograph of himself that was disturbing him. There were orbs all around Mitch, along with all these weird fuzzy things I had never seen before. I took the photo to the one and only good witch of the south, my paranormal hostess with the mostess, Janine. Straight off the bat, she said that there was nothing supernatural about the photograph and that there was something in Mitch's clothing that was giving off a shine to give that orby sort of look. Even my husband, Ross, who is far from being a psychic, had said the same thing. Off I went to another friend who said it had something to do with Mitch's work. I just couldn't make anything of it as Mitch is a good friend and I found myself too personally involved to not have a biased eye. Although I must admit, it didn't really feel as though he had some Spirit activity around him having a house party at his expense.

So, in walked Greg and asked what we were looking at. Straight away, he needed to vibe. I am not sure why, but I think the theatrics helped him get to the point a bit better. Then came the talking in tongues, and I was like, "really?" Then, just like the lightning bolt that struck Dr Emmett in "Back to the Future," Greg received an answer from the highest, ascended master, twice removed cousin from the

121

Prophet Abraham and a distant relative to Jesus Christ. He stopped us all, and with bated breath and trying not to laugh, we waited patiently for the words to come out of his mouth – "aliens," he said. Yes, aliens. Don't get me wrong; I do enjoy a bit of ET conspiracy myself, but this particular day there was no way, no how any extra-terrestrial interference was having its way with my good ole Aussie tradie mate, Mitch. We were sternly warned by Greg, amidst absolute silence, not to go anywhere near Mitch ever again, for we did not want to meet the same fate of an alien encounter as this mere mortal.

I guess you want to know what the orbs were, after all? We did some tests, and, after a bit of detective work, we found out that it did have something to do with Mitch's work clothing. He works in the mines in South Australia, and the material in his work clothes would give off this glare that makes it look like pure ghostly interference. All Mitch's workmates had the same thing going on in their photographs too. And guess what happened to my old mate Greg? He is now charging people $800 to clear any ghosts, spirits, aliens, and god knows what else from people's homes. Apparently, the Shamans from ancient times have entered his body (which we call walk-ins), and for an extra few hundred, he will also heal you as well.

All I can say is thank fuck for the Janines of this world who don't charge a thing for their house clearing work and the Colins who spend their time healing and praying for people, asking for nothing in return!

I was invited to a club show a few years ago in which I took along a few friends. The psychic on stage was reading people like a book, and, being the sceptical psychic that I am, I needed to do some detective work. I looked and scanned the room until I found her friend. These friends are always easy to find. They are ones with earpieces that are so tiny you can hardly see them. In fact, you won't actually see them because, in the first place, you are not trained to look for them like I am. So, while the audience is mingling, the psychic's mule is doing some investigating of their own. It is more than likely that you have seen this in the movies where the psychic (or in the movie's case, it's usually the evangelistic pastor) is being fed the information by their spy directly into their earpiece.

I can't tell you how many times I have seen this, and yes, I apologise because I, too, have been guilty of being the mule. In my defence, however, I did not realise that I was being played until the show was over. I was asked by a friend who was on stage if I would mingle with her audience for a while; during that time, she was still preparing herself in the dressing room. I was then called over to the dresser and asked if I could now help sell tickets at the door and make sure I was questioning all the guests as to what they were hoping to get out of that evening's sessions. Innocently, I thought I was helping out a mate, but it was not until after the show I realised exactly what was going on. As my friend called me into her dresser to help with her zip, she casually got all the information out of me about the audience who were walking through the door. In usual Rosie form, I innocently gave away all the information this psychic needed to put on the show of their life! I sunk deeper and deeper into my chair as the show was progressing, embarrassed and humiliated that I had been used as a pawn, and I didn't even know it. Word for word of what I relayed back to my friend was said out loud once she had become the psychic on the stage, and I cringed every time I heard somebody say, "Wow." This performance earned my friend (who is no longer my friend) a very big acknowledgement in the psychic field, which included their very own TV show and a stupid certificate by a made-up organisation to claim them the leader of the psychic industry. To this day, I cannot bear to watch her show as I feel sick knowing that I was part of the problem and that I had helped create yet another absolute egotistical, boastful, bragging, conceited, and totally full of themselves "celebrity" psychic.

Another psychic I worked with for some time made international headlines when they were able to guess who was being eliminated each week from a popular American TV show. The show had contestants being chosen to stay on an extra week whilst one was always asked to leave. Everyone raved about this psychic's ability to the extent that they now charge well over $1,000 for a reading, and stupid people pay for it. Whilst this psychic was staying at my home for a few weeks whilst looking for another place to move into, my "psychic" friend received a phone call. By this stage, she had started to make her name known amongst well-known personalities, and they fell in love with her engaging charm and free readings. You see, a little bit of "Googling" a celebrity's profile is always a good tool for a fake psychic. Anyway, back to the phone call my friend received from a contestant on the well-known show. I was there at my dinner table, and the contestant, being a close friend of my friend's, was relaying to her all about the filming of the show, as it was pre-filmed months before it aired. The contestant even told my friend who was leaving and who was staying. I think my friend forgot about this night, as she had her friend on loudspeaker, and Ross and I had heard every bit of their conversation. Many months later, when the show did air, you can imagine everybody's surprise that an Australian psychic knew exactly who was winning and who was not before it actually came on TV. Ross always tells me that I was the silly one, as I should have predicted the fate of the contestants and made myself the talk of the town. People with no conscience can do that; people like me cannot.

In our psychic world, it is very hard to tell who is faking their way to success. With Google being your number one tool, it is easy to get all the information you need on a client. But when that client is not on Google, all you need to do is pick up on some body language, and boom, you have just won the jackpot. There are so many wannabes who have made it to celebrity status in our industry, and I feel that social media is to blame for this. For some reason, we as humans like to make insecure and troubled people ridiculously famous and feel better by putting our fate into somebody else's hands. Before social media, I don't recall seeing every Tom, Dick, and Harry becoming a psychic. Now it runs rampant, and I am just embarrassed.

Believe me when I say I have worked with hundreds of psychics over the 30 years of my career. I have also worked with some amazing ones who I call the 'real deal,' and they seem to have something the fake ones do not. They do not care about their image or the money they make. They genuinely want to make a difference in their clients' lives, and with that, the money always comes. Embrace once hosted a celebrity psychic who predicted on national television the fate of the missing Malaysian MH370. I had this strong gut feeling it was in the water, but our celebrity went on to convince the crowd it had been abducted by Russian spies. I vowed never to have this man back in our store again after he bragged about how much he is always 100 per cent right with his predictions and how the paparazzi were following him around everywhere he went. (Eye roll is inserted here). I will be the first to tell you that no psychic can ever be that correct, and if they were, they would not be hosting talks in crystal shops like ours. I felt embarrassed for him after evidence and pieces of the plane were found in the water. But I felt a little sad when years later I came across a YouTube clip where he was seen as a fraud and being made fun of along with some other well-known fake psychics.

A student of mine once rang me to ask if my husband, Ross, could give her some information on the football season as she had been chosen to pick the winners for the games on our local radio program. She had no idea about football and needed a footy fan's perspective on the game and who was likely to win the grand finale. Ross gave his input based solely on which team was holding the highest score all throughout the season. Listening to the psychic's predictions that night both Ross and I laughed as we heard my husband's words being repeated word for word in the psychic's interview. Surely enough, the team he predicted did win, and the psychic never spoke to either of us again. I did, however, shake my head to the point of dizziness when she told people that her newfound football information came from her sporty spirit guides and not my husband, Ross.

I was introduced to an extremely well known and famous American psychic who I had seen on many TV documentaries and shows. Admittedly, I really thought they had a very special and talented gift, and I was beside myself when they offered to give me a free reading. I couldn't wait for days until the phone call came, and I had all the questions I wanted to ask neatly written down on a writing pad beside my phone. After our pleasantries, comparing each other's weather and time differences, they went straight into the reading by telling me that I was a famous queen long ago in India. Those very first words turned me off the whole reading as I knew first of all I wasn't, and secondly, when you get told you were someone super famous and influential from the past, that there was no way I was coming back as the person I am today.

I was then told I would never find love, and I would spend my days alone and single with no children. I married Ross a few years later, and with six children between us, I have my very own Brady Bunch. I was also told that I would close Embrace and live in England, where I would live in the country, drink tea all day, and live off my land. Not only is Embrace well and truly thriving these days, I don't like the cold weather, and I am a city girl who likes to drink coffee and could never imagine living far from my family. Obviously, I was so disappointed. Not because I didn't like what was being told to me, but because of how I had built this psychic up to a point I could have sworn they were the next Messiah. I promised myself that day that I would become a lot more discerning and not so fooled by another TV psychic ever again.

I met Sharina Star many years ago. We also worked together at Embrace's FESTIVAL OF DREAMS event. She is one of the country's most celebrated psychics, and instantly, I knew in our first meeting that she was my double, a sister from another mister. Both of us dressed in leopard print, bling from ear to toe, and both sporting bright red nails and lipstick to match; it was like we had known each other our entire lives. I knew who Sharina was as I frequently listened to her radio show on Sunday nights, and I had seen her in various TV shows and movies. In my eyes, Sharina was down to earth and a lot of fun but it wasn't the fame itself that made her popular amongst her clients; it was the love and care she gave them even though she had celebrity status. I enjoyed watching her stage shows as she made sure her audience was having fun while she added in a bit of cheek and a heap of laughter. Sharina didn't offer serious readings on the stage, and she refused to talk to the dead (as she would refer to it) because she always believed that psychics had a responsibility to their clients, especially while they are mourning. As she mentored me over the years, we grew closer and closer as our morals matched, and so did our wardrobes.

The one thing I had admired about her is that Sharina holds a diploma in counselling and psychology with high distinctions to boot, and also with a private eye master's degree. She knows first-hand how to deal with people in agony, and she actually cared. I learnt a lot from her over the years, and I learnt that two women could most definitely be in the same industry with no competition between them while enjoying a true and solid friendship.

I've been lucky to meet other Sharinas over the years, but sadly they are far and few between in the field that I work in. Hours upon hours, we would talk and compare notes on our lives whilst enjoying a glass of champagne in one hand and a phone in the other. I owe a lot of my public profile to Sharina, as she helped me push my barriers and stand like a tall poppy in a field full of weeds. It is also really nice to have someone you can bounce off every now and then with ideas and future projects without having to walk away whilst taking the knives out of my back.

Sharina made international headlines when she said in an interview to the Daily Mail that she is a sceptical psychic and believes that some psychics are fake. Sharina didn't agree with the psychics who rort vulnerable people, as she believes that people make wrong decisions and wrong choices when they are grieving. The article went viral, and within days, her phone rang non-stop from people all around the world wanting readings from her.

Have you ever heard of the Forer Effect? It's the same thing as those silly Facebook quizzes we always fall for (well, I do anyway). We know deep down that these quizzes are just for fun, but we like to believe that the personality descriptions it gives about ourselves apply directly to us. Do you get me? It's a well-known phenomenon used in psychology and sometimes is also referred to as the Barnum Effect. Even though the description actually can apply to everyone and anyone, the subject still insists that it can only apply to them and only them. It's a little like that with psychic readings. I know I am not going to make many friends here amongst my peers, but it's a fact, and even the best of the best psychics have been guilty of using this method, even if they don't necessarily believe they are doing so. Or perhaps, they don't even know that they are doing so.

There was once a showman by the name of PT Barnum, who said that "A sucker is born every minute," and hence that is where the name came from. So, when a psychic starts to give common knowledge that could apply to everyone, the client becomes gullible, believing that the information is just for them, no matter how generic it actually is.

For me, and from my own experiences with psychics, I believe that people can be convinced that this information is solely for them because they so badly want to hear something good in their lives. They also do not want to know that perhaps they were just fooled into spending lots of money on the reading. This style of reading makes the client feel extremely special, unique, and highly susceptible to any other information that is about to come. I mean, if they can get this bit of generic knowledge right then, that means the rest of the reading has to be right too. Are you getting the drift here?

Everybody in this world needs a little bit of hope in their lives, and I have found that some of the most popular and busiest psychics are the ones that can offer that to their clients. I only have to happen to walk past our reading rooms at Embrace to hear the conversations that are going on between the psychics and their clients. In no way am I eavesdropping, but it is hard not to hear, and I have worked out the pattern as to why some readers are very popular and some are not. I guess you could call it a party trick, where the psychic can easily fool you into believing they have access to these wonderful insights about your life and doing it in such a way that you would have no clue that you have just been fooled. A great psychic is somebody who will tell you what you want to hear, and each time you nod your head in agreement, it makes it easier for the reader to pick up on the next cues. Anyone can do it; in fact, we all do it in everyday life; we just don't realise we are doing this. Once the psychic gets the hook in, the rest is easy.

The many statements that come from the psychic's mouth can be so ambiguous that they can be true for you, for me, for the neighbours you have never met that live down the road, and even for good old Father Christmas! Let me give you an example. I once knew a psychic who was booked out 12 months ahead and could not keep up with the demand of clients that were at her doorstep day and night. She complained to me that she had no life left and that her husband was getting upset by the lack of personal time they shared together. I knew her style of reading well as she always bragged about how she could and would tell her clients everything they wanted to hear. I overheard her one day in the midst of a reading, and she was explaining to her client that, at times, she can see this woman getting so stressed out to the point she feels that no one understands her. Of course, the client is going to think this psychic is amazing because guess what? It is true! It is true for the client, it is true for me, and it is definitely true for you; we all have some stress at times and feel like the world just doesn't understand us. It's a fact of being a human.

I have to tell you I get really annoyed with vague readings. I've seen it over and over again when the psychic claims to hear a name starting with S. My sister Sarah starts with S, so does my sister-in-law, Stacey. Oh, and my next-door neighbour Sue also starts with an S. Then there is my best friend's dog, Sally. See what I mean? I think that if a Spirit was going to give you a name, they wouldn't just stop at the first letter. They made it thus far to convey some information to you; they might as well finish the name off. So, if you reply that the S name is your husband, Steve, you usually will get something back like, "Oh, of course, it is. I knew it had something to do with someone on your husband's side." Now the psychic knows you have a husband, and the rest is fair game.

"I have old man Bob here with me, and he is telling me that he died of heart disease." Just stop for a moment and think to yourself. How many men do you know with the name Bob or the letter B? Now tell me, how many men you know who have died of heart disease? And if you don't know this person, it's easy, the person sitting behind you will. And if they don't, then, of course, the psychic, along with all his theatrics, is receiving too many dead loved ones in his head at once, so it must be the woman in the very first row sitting over there. Easy isn't it?

In psychic lingo, this is called a cold reading. Basically, it is a technique in which the mediums will ask a whole heap of general questions, and then they rely on the verbal and physical cues to extract personal information from their victim, oops, I mean client. A hot reading is one that involves researching the people who are going to be in the room beforehand and using the details from the Facebook or Instagram accounts, or even LinkedIn to use in the readings. Without getting myself into any trouble here, we once hosted a very well-known International psychic at our home for a few days who admitted to me that this was the best and most accurate way he found out information about his client. This is the very same psychic medium who has been interviewed by some of the most prominent names in the chat show industry and the very same man who has fraud charges against his name. Oh, he is also the very same spiritual guru who dated a friend of ours once, and Ross was made to get out of bed at 2 in the morning to rescue our friend from a very bad case of domestic violence. I am not quite sure how he is still around performing the same old tricks, but he is now a psychic to the celebrities, which somehow makes him better than the rest of us.

I have a belief that because the client has just paid an extraordinary amount of money to see the psychic, they subconsciously need to believe that their psychic is good and somehow convince themselves of such. It is a bit of a blow to the ego to realise you have just been conned out of a few hundred dollars, so people will always hear what they want to hear. It is so much easier to keep the reading vague because that way, it allows the psychic to backtrack on anything they may have missed. A client's body language will always give you a clue to your next move. It only takes a subtle shift in their chair, a facial expression or even a fidgety smile and that is all that is needed to give the psychic a hint of where they are to go next.

I once asked a very popular reader at Embrace how she has become so well-known and what her secret is. Her reply was not what I was expecting but something I will never forget. I found her telling me that clients will nod when she has picked up on something correct or shake their heads if not. That way, she is always one step ahead of knowing the direction that the reading is going to take. When I look back at some of my readings, I can recall that she was correct. Many times, clients would nod in agreement or shake with hesitation, and without realising it, their reaction would make the reading so much more fluid.

Do yourself a favour and go find Keith Barry on TED talks. He is a famous magician and entertainer, and his talk is probably one of the best I have ever listened to. He mysteriously managed to find out the name of a woman's ex-boyfriend who was sitting in the audience without her saying much of a word. Even though Keith Barry doesn't give away the secrets to his tricks, what he does try to do is express how his audience gives him more information with their reactions and body language.

One thing I have learnt over the years of doing thousands of readings is that people absolutely love hearing about themselves and share information without them even knowing they are doing so. There were many times I have had to ask my client to stop talking as their words were getting me confused with the actual messages I was channelling. However, there had been times when I just couldn't connect with someone. It happens to every good psychic. Sometimes our energies just don't gel, or sometimes we just don't get anything and we cannot connect no matter what. The important thing to remember when this does happen is that a real psychic will tell you the truth, that they are just not getting a proper connection. A fake psychic will not tell you and go on to do a reading and insist that everything they are saying is true even though none of it really makes sense. I cannot even begin to tell you how many times I have seen that the client is shaking their head in disagreement and the psychic is insisting that their dead aunt, who is very much alive, is passing on messages.

Another point I would like to add is if a psychic tells you that you or your family have a curse or a hex or some black magic or voodoo or a spell put on you, then RUN! I do not believe in such things, and I sadly had to fire a psychic at Embrace because I found out that is how she was able to keep herself so booked out week after week. Fear can do a lot to a respectable and smart person, and bad luck is a part of life along with all the good luck we receive also. It's a cycle and this too shall pass. As soon as a client believes they have had some bad luck put on them in some manner, they are easily manipulated into spending some big dollars for the psychic to remove it for them. I am going to let you in on a little secret... if you believe you do have a curse of some sort on you, all you need to do is pray. It is as easy as that, and it is free. We are not praying for the curse to be lifted, however, as there never was a curse, to begin with, we are praying to be released from the person who is evil enough and cocky enough to believe they have such power. It is a scam, and these people will sell you enough snake oil they can con you into, even if it is a few hundred dollars to cleanse your home. Nobody has any power over you to place a curse or to lift a curse, so always remember that you once again just need to tap your shiny red shoes and remember that you had the power all along, my dear.

Let's face a fact; most people come to psychics when they are most vulnerable. I can attest to this as a reader myself and as the owner of Embrace, which I can proudly say now hosts one hundred per cent real deal readers. It took me a while, though, to sift through them all and perhaps that is why I gave myself a reputation of an unfair boss but a loyal and ethical one at the same time. There is not one client who can say they were exploited by me or Embrace at any time, and instead, as professionals, we have referred them to proper channels, whether it is their doctor, psychologist or counsellor. A true psychic is a professional in their field, and a counsellor is a professional in theirs. It becomes very dangerous when both the psychic and their client mix up the two. This is why we have a rule at Embrace that we do not see the same client twice in a short period of time and we have a referral system whereby our psychics must, at all times, pass on emergency phone numbers. This ensures that the proper and responsible trained people have taken over and the client is placed into the right hands.

Many years ago, a client of mine, Dixie, would threaten to kill herself if I would not read for her. She became addicted to psychic readings, and that addiction came through so clearly in our readings. If she didn't hear what she wanted to hear, she would easily move onto the next reader and then the next. She would have no hesitation in ringing us during the dark of the night or early morning, asking question after question such as whether Nash would come back to her. She became more than obsessed, and somehow, I started to feel like I was living in the movie 'Single White Female.' We had to very softly hold an intervention with her on one particular Saturday afternoon as my other readers were also uncomfortable with her behaviour. She had been stalking a man who was clearly not interested in her, and she had sneakily booked in three different session readings that day under different aliases. We had to be very careful how we approached her as she, in my eyes, was not mentally stable. We told her that a psychic was not what she needed and referred her to a clinical counsellor. With that, she stormed out of my store and placed some very bad and awful reviews about Embrace and our readers. So instead of moving on to see the correct professional who really would have helped her, she opened her own psychic shop with plenty of readers working for her where she could have had all the psychic readings she wanted. Last I heard, she too became a psychic!

What was sad about Dixie is that other than her obsessive-compulsive personality when it came to this man, and her addiction to readings, I believe she had a lot of potential to have given herself a really great life and meet the love she so desperately desired. Because she would not let Nash go, she was not making room for the next man to enter her life. I think about her often and I hope that she did get the right help she needed as no one should have to feel the pain so badly that it becomes not only an expensive addiction but a dangerous one at that.

After working with hundreds of psychics over the years, I must admit I have noticed that mental health issues can run rampant. From my observations, their pain runs so deep that they want to put themselves in a position to help others, but I also believe that they need to help themselves first. I have also worked with psychics who come from backgrounds of domestic abuse, who are alcohol and drug dependant, whose grown children want nothing to do with them, readers who do not have $2.00 to buy themselves a cup of tea or get themselves a bus ticket home. And yet, these very same people are giving advice on becoming rich or standing in your own power and leaving the marriage because the husband does not put the toilet seat down.

I've worked with psychics who have never found love in their life and yet they are preaching the same to their clients; psychics whose need to become famous outweighs anything they do because they don't get the adoration and applause they so badly need at home. I've been to psychics' homes where they are so unhygienic, and yet they want to preach about the light and how to get your health and home in order. I've been in conversation with psychics where they detest their stepchildren so much that they would rather feed them poison apples than to have them in the same room, and yet these are the very same people who are on stage preaching kindness and love. I've been in enough psychic circles to know that if these men and women can bitch the way they just had about someone who thinks they are their friend, then I know that they will do the same with me as soon as my back is turned. And yet, these are the very same spiritual, loving psychics who can make you feel like a million dollars when you are with them and like a piece of trash when you are not. There are psychics who have once worked for me at Embrace such that I have taken time out to look after their children in order for them to work, have fed them in my home, and snuck a few extra dollars into their pay to help them get through their week. The very same psychics would steal clients from Embrace, money from my till, and stock from my shelves and have affairs with each other's husbands. These very same 'spiritual' people can no longer say a mere 'hello' if they pass by me in the street. It's all a contradiction, nothing but smoke and mirrors! My advice is to do your homework and do it well.

I totally agree that most of the time, a person will come in for a reading at a low point in their life and will walk out feeling just fine. I do not see the harm in selling them some hope. The world needs hope, hope is my favourite word, and I believe in hope. I have seen it work its magic day in and day out, and if hope can put a smile on somebody's face, then my work is done. I believe it is fair to sell hope to a client once, but to sell it to them repeatedly is a dog-eat-dog game and does not sit within my scope of integrity and honesty. An honest psychic will never try to target you when the chips are down, and you are in a vulnerable place of uncertainty. I especially feel this dishonesty is rampant with the telephone and television psychic hotlines, but we shall cover that in another chapter later on.

Chapter 8

Run Sister Run

"Be the woman who fixes another woman's crown without telling the world it was broken."

A wise man once said, "Show me your friends and I will tell you who you are." An even wiser one by the name of Colin would always tell me that you see a person's true colours when you are no longer beneficial to them. It took me thirty years to learn this and I had my heart torn into pieces in the process.

Bodie and I became good friends back in the good ol' days before social media, fame whores, and celebrity psychics. We would always share a cheeky giggle at the wannabes and some of the crap that would come out of their mouths. Those were fun days, as the psychic world was still innocent and hadn't yet been raped by egos and money. Bodie saw it like I did, and we were on the same wavelength until the day she gifted me over $3000 worth of crystals as a present for the inauguration of Embrace.

Although I was ecstatic as they were amazing pieces, I did find the gift hard to accept as it was too expensive. Bodie promised me that she no longer needed these babies, and some of the jewellery pieces still had their original tags on them. I was astounded by her generosity, and I insisted on paying her, but she wouldn't have any of that. We placed the crystals very strategically on our shelves and filled our windows and cabinets. I remember feeling so grateful for having such amazing friends in my life. I tried to pay back Bodie by taking her for lunches, gifting her with new stock that would come in and just by being a good friend to her when she needed a shoulder to lean on. I even went as far as buying her groceries, as what she had gifted me was a whole lot more than $3000 when you took the retail value into consideration.

Like all the crystals in our store, it didn't take long to sell them, and Bodie had offered to bring more as she had plenty from wherever those had come from. I couldn't believe how kind Bodie was until a new staff member overheard our conversation and took me aside for a little chat. You see, she had worked with Bodie in a previous employment, and even though I was led to believe Bodie had left on her own terms, it seems she had been asked to leave her previous employment because she had been caught stealing from the warehouse and putting her hand in the cash register a few times too many. It was hard for me to believe that my gorgeous friend would be capable of such a crime, and I needed some time to process this information.

It took me a while to register what was being said, and the enormity of being an unwilling participant in the theft was a tough one to process. I felt sick, I felt stressed, and I had quite a panic attack. I had no choice but to confront Bodie, and I remember what a horrible position I had found myself in, as I truly and honestly believed that the gifted crystals were hers. I had no reason to doubt her until she became hysterical when I questioned her. She practically foamed at the mouth as she grabbed her coat and bag and stormed out of Embrace, cursing as she did so. I cried because I didn't know what else to do.

Needless to say, I thought that was the end of Bodie until that night when Celina and I stayed back at Embrace to merchandise the jewellery cabinets. Now, I really need you to be sitting down for what is about to come next because to this day, I still find it terrifying and unbelievable. Let's just say that Celina is a vision of beauty, someone you could easily find on the cover of Vogue. Men threw themselves at her, and women felt very insecure around her perfect face and stunning looks. Celina was the kind of girl you could not dislike, as her personality was just as beautiful as her face. She and I were working on the Friday that Bodie had theatrically left. In the dead silence of the night, a piece of Bodie's jewellery flew right off our shelf where we had collected the lot to return to her. It made a loud thumping noise. Celina looked at me, and I at her, and we were like, "What the fuck? How did that happen?" We didn't give it much thought until a few minutes later, a mirror we had for sale, hanging on the wall, with the most immaculate carvings of Medussa, came flying off the hook that held it in place. It flew straight towards Celina. Glass was everywhere, it shattered into millions of pieces and the hook that held the mirror was still firmly in place. It was at that moment, I knew straight away that we were under a psychic attack. It is interesting how in Greek mythology, Athena's jealousy turned Medusa into what we know today as the woman with snakes in her hair, and it is also interesting that Bodie's jealousy of Celina was targeted directly at her. Coincidence? I think not.

It didn't take long for word to get around that Embrace was selling stolen crystals. Bodie had started a rumour that she knew would not stop in our ever gossiping "spiritual" community but instead would keep getting bigger and bigger. I guess you want to know what happened to the stolen crystals? I was able to find the rightful owner, and because of my honesty, they too gifted them back to me. Karma can be a beautiful thing sometimes.

I guess there is a loophole in working with the supernatural, and that loophole is that you can't really tell if someone is truly gifted or not, as there is no way to prove it. It also means that you cannot tell if someone is coming from the dark or the light, as the dark always has a way of knowing your weaknesses and having some fun with them.

If another psychic in our industry calls me her 'sister' ever again, I think I will just scream and then run, or run and then scream, or just do both right at the very same time. It is a phrase you will regularly hear amongst our psychic community and one that I truly believe is taken in vain.

A 'sister' came to work with us when we were working on the Festival of Dreams, and we had brought in some very prominent Native American Hollywood movie stars. The event caused a media frenzy as it was the first time that indigenous Americans had come to speak about their culture on Australian soil. Danicha couldn't wait to come on board and be a part of what was about to make Australian history.

It was a rainy Sunday morning, and we had organized a press release and PR event to be held right alongside Sydney's iconic Harbour Bridge. Aboriginal elders came to pay their respects to their American brothers, and to this day, I get goosebumps when I look back at the enormity of what we had pulled off. Danicha couldn't stop thanking me for allowing her to spend one-on-one time with her hero, and she would repeatedly tell me that she loved me like a sister and how we were soul family and all that other rubbish that people in our industry tell you. She loved me, we were meant to be friends forever and blah blah blah. However, she didn't love me enough when we had the TV station cameras filming a ceremony we had organized, and she somehow ended up in all the photos pretending to be me. Not only had she taken my clothes to wear, she told the film crew to film when my back was turned, and I missed out on my own event!

I was furious. Not because I wanted to be in the limelight in the photos, but because we had no intention of not including Danicha in any of them. I was gutted and felt beyond sick that someone could pull off a stunt like that in broad daylight and think nothing of it. Sister, my backside! For the rest of that week, whilst we were hosting our international guests, Danicha was eerily trying to be me and mimicking everything I was doing and wearing. I started to feel like I was once again in the movie 'Single White Female,' and I had to sit her down and gently break the news to her that she needed to be none other than herself and allow me the space to be me.

The big day of the festival arrived, and it was time for me to go on stage to express my appreciation at the inauguration of the event with a Welcome to the Country by our indigenous elders. I had a special outfit all planned out and left it hanging in a green room behind the stage, nicely ironed so that I could just quickly throw it on and duck back onto the stage. When I went to get it, it wasn't there, and I found myself retracing my steps in order to make sure I did indeed pack it with my other belongings. There was no time to waste, and I ran onto the stage in what I was already wearing. What I was supposed to have been wearing, however, was staring at me in the face as Danicha, in all her glory, sat in the very front row, in my very clothes! It was then that I knew this had gone beyond being creepy, and once again, I had to become the bad guy and tell Danicha that her actions were just not acceptable. To further rub salt into my wounds, I had spent $600 on a few outfits for Danicha as I genuinely wanted to give her a new wardrobe of her own, knowing that she was financially struggling and could not afford to buy herself some nice new clothes.

As it was the last day of our event, I never heard from Danicha again. She blocked me on social media but not before leaving a trail of nasty gossip, utter lies, and complete bullshit about me. She deleted over six hundred emails in my database alongside a huge list of potential clients for our next event. She even deleted over a thousand photos that were taken throughout the festival so that I would not have access to any. She called me sister, however, I had other names for her by the time our event had finished.

Last I heard, Danicha was teaching people how to heal themselves and practising hypnotherapy on them. Oh, and she was also another one of those life/psychic

/meditation /coaches, you know the ones? The ones with the certificates! Need I say more?

A well-known Australian psychic would call me regularly just to touch base and see how Embrace was going. In each and every phone call, he couldn't help but bring himself to talk down a friend of his who adored the life out of him. She would constantly put pictures on her social media of both of them together, and he would bitch about her behind her back with as much consistency. I knew that if he could talk about her like that, then he might also be doing the same with me. I felt sad for her as she truly adored him and believed he was a good mate. My last words many years ago to him were that I didn't want to hear any more of his nasty gossip, and so he turned his tongue on me. Every now and then, I still see the pretty pictures of him and his friend on social media with captions of how much they love each other. If only she knew.

Another 'sister' of mine loved me so much until the day came when I could no longer be of use to her. It was a ten-year friendship that manifested because of our mutual love for crystals and, unbeknownst to me, because of the contacts I could put her in touch with. I understand that sometimes friendships fade and that we sadly move in different directions, but I will never understand how and why people, especially in the spiritual world (or any other world), can be so mean to each other.

Being a woman and being betrayed by another woman hurts so deeply, especially when an element of cruelty is attached to it. As I write, I shed some tears because I find myself still grieving the loss of someone I held so dear, a woman whom I loved from the very bottom of my heart, and a friend I was proud to call my sister. One day there was intimacy and trust, and the next, there was not. I don't think a day went by when we weren't on the phone with each other, sharing our deepest secrets. We shared our wounds over coffee, wine, dinners, work and picnics, and there was nothing that I would not have done for that woman. Our friendship was like a marriage, and I had found my female other half. We were close, we were tight, and together, we were unstoppable. This was until the day she stopped taking my calls and acknowledging my presence.

There is a thing they call 'ghosting,' and as a psychic, I think she spent so much time on the other side of the ethers that she literally had become a ghost. In my world anyway.

Phone calls after phone calls were never answered, messages not read, and I was not only being deleted but blocked on all social media channels, which made it even harder for me to find out what on earth the issue was. At first, I didn't think there was anything wrong and assumed that her disappearance meant that she had been super busy. I was right, she was super busy, busy with going behind my back and doing something so despicable that heartbroken is not even the word to describe how heartbroken I had become.

For some reason, I hesitate to write much about my 'sister.' Perhaps it's still raw for me, and perhaps I still hope that one day she will come back to me and not only apologise but explain how she was so in my face one day and easily disappeared the next. I guess deep down inside, I still want to hold a protective layer over her, and I struggle to say a bad word about her as I truly have none.

I searched for answers from mutual friends, and the pain I felt whenever her name came up in conversation would have me running to the bathroom with that nervous poo feeling, my stomach rumbling, and my nerves shaking. Ross, my husband, had warned me about her a long time ago; Colin had warned me the very first time he had met her, and so had Helen. I didn't listen. I didn't even have a gut feeling about this one, so I can't help but wonder if together she and I needed to pay back some karma from a lifetime long ago and a memory long forgotten.

She wanted to hurt me, but she broke me instead. I suffered in silence when in public, but at home, when I was in the loving arms of my husband, I cried for nights on end, wondering how I could have changed things and what it was that I had done to make her so mad at me. I would go over and over our conversations to see if there was something, just anything I may have said to have upset her in a way that would justify such hatred. I couldn't find any.

Mutual friends tried to cheer me up, but I could see in their faces that they knew the truth, that they, too, had heard whatever it was she had said about me and that they were placed in a horrible predicament. We shared the same circle of 'sisters,' and we shared the same careers; hell, at one stage, we even shared each other's clothes and cars. We would joke that we would share anything and everything with each other except our husbands, and we would always find ourselves giggling like school girls whenever we found ourselves saying it. She ended our friendship in a cruel and harsh manner with no consideration that such a heartless move would devastate a big softie like me. Or did she? She wanted to hurt me, and I will never know why. The pain ran so deep that I found myself consulting psychics to find out what on earth was going on. They all told me the same thing, that jealousy has a way of tearing friendships apart.

She took some friends along with her, and honestly, I was glad to say goodbye to them, but she never once had the integrity, the balls, or the scruples to tell me what it was that I had done wrong. She knew me better than anyone, and she knew this would make me crumble. I did crumble for a while. This woman always spoke about standing in your power, and yet her actions showed me nothing but cowardliness and weakness. She couldn't even confront me with whatever her issue was because doing so meant that she would have to admit that she was the one in the wrong.

I have heard a lot of untrue things said about me from my former BFF, but I came to realise that you can always tell who the strong women are, and they are ones you will see building one another up instead of tearing them down.

Whenever my kids are fighting, I always quote this saying, "Do you want to be right or do you want to be happy?" I really didn't care who was right or wrong. If it was me that was in the wrong, I was open to rectifying my mistake. As humans, there are times when we upset another person without even knowing it or meaning it. If this was one of those times, bring it on, tell me about it so I could ensure it would never happen again. But, this story didn't end like that. It ended in a way where a lot of people felt they needed to take sides. Once they did, I noticed a great divide, and it reminded me of that time in the Bible when Jesus' followers cheered him on Palm Sunday and crucified him the following week. A bit like the 6 of wands in the tarot, but this time my Judas came in the form of a best friend. It wasn't a nice way to go out, especially when somebody got their kicks from the pain they were inflicting.

Our society is judged by how we treat our weakest members, and at the time, I was being ghosted by my best friend. I was also going through the darkest night of my life. My insecurities were played upon, and my kindness preyed on. If she could do this to me, I wonder what she could do to all her clients who pay her big dollars to coach them, give them psychic counselling, and show them how to become better people in this world. Ironic, isn't it?

I truly believed that our friendship would stand the test of time and that she was completely loyal to me. It took me a long time to realise that in the 'spiritual' industry, a lot of people are only loyal to their need of you, and their loyalty changes once their needs change. We were the best of friends, or at least that is what I had thought, and her silence hurt me more than any foe had ever hurt me. A severed friendship can be as painful as a break-up, and along with the memories and experiences you hold with that person, it can be excruciating. I was used. Embrace became the stepping stone for her to climb the ladder of success, and I became the sucker who held her hair back when she was vomiting, stayed up till all hours of the night listening to how she was in a loveless relationship. I had her back right up to the end, even when she stole customers from under my nose (something I chose to turn a blind eye to).

I hope that nobody reading this book ever has to experience the feelings of hurt and betrayal that I experience whenever her name pops up in certain circles. What makes it harder is that a lot of people idolise her and think of her as some magical priestess. If only they knew.

It takes a long time to deal with the devastation of losing someone you always thought you would have by your side. When our friendship ended, I kept looking back and questioning our entire relationship and wondering where I had gone wrong. I now find myself focusing on how our friendship fulfiled us while it lasted and what I had to learn from it. I had to eventually move on from a place of gratitude. To lose a dear friend in this manner is very painful and leaves a hole in your life that can never be filled the same way ever again. I just didn't expect it to be someone who was supposed to be so spiritual and kind.

I found myself in a situation where somebody I loved from the depths of my soul was knowingly, intentionally, and with malevolent intent had done me dirty, and was hoping for the worst possible outcome for the business that had kept food on her table for so long.

The wind out of my sails had been knocked out, and the person I trusted, who I thought had my back, who I had always been there for, thought that she would break me and thought that she could do things to me that she believed would keep me down. Instead, I bounced back, it took a while, but I did. I had no other choice. Here is the thing about

162

people like this in your life, people who think they have a power over you to break you, to have a superpower where they can put a spell or curse over you, and where it feels like life as you know it is falling apart. Guess what? It is falling apart, only for it to fall back together again, just this time, they are not in it.

Another "sister" of mine came to visit Embrace in our early days and happened to leave us a present. It was a rusted needle threaded with brown cotton that had knots all the way through it. At first glance, one of my staff thought it was nothing, but after one look, I knew it was a "hex." You see, this sister could not stand the thought that Embrace was becoming an entity within itself, a force to be reckoned with, and so she thought it in her best interest to put a curse on the shop in order for us to close down. Truth always has a way of coming out, and it took two years for us to find out that someone I loved dearly, who I held close to my heart and who received huge discounts at Embrace, was the sister who did this to us.

Once again, I called upon Janine and my girlfriend Effie to come to the rescue. Later that night, when the shops were all closed and we were all alone in the shopping centre, we began our cleansing ritual. Effie brought in some amazing-smelling homegrown herbs to burn, and I insisted that the staff also attend the ceremony. My sister (the real one with the same mother), who actually finds herself freaking out about this sort of stuff, insisted on joining, and I am glad that she did. Sometimes you need the eyes of a non-believer to see for themselves, therefore, convincing you that it is not all just in your head.

We placed our positive affirmations for Embrace onto white paper, which we started to slowly burn in the cauldron. The only problem was that the paper refused to burn, and in the process of waiting and waiting, the heat from the cauldron slowly started to burn through the wooden floorboards underneath it. I leaned into the cauldron to give it a stir, and with a loud hiss of a snake, the flame rose to my height and formed the head of a serpent. It went straight for me, and I jumped back just as the flame attached itself to my black cotton dress. They say that snakes don't hiss anymore, instead, they call you babe, bro or friend, but this time my snake did both.

Janine quickly placed the lid on the cauldron whilst my sister threw the contents of her bottled water on me, and with that, the serpent went back to where it came from. My sister spoke about this for a long time afterwards as she admits that she would not have believed it if she hadn't seen it firsthand for herself. The girls wanted me to do a binding ritual so that the perpetrator could not perform any more of her black magic on the shop or me. Instead, I chose to play innocent, and ten years on, I still see this woman occasionally in the shopping centre. She doesn't know that I know, and somehow, I get much delight in the look on her face when she sees that we are still in business. I killed her with kindness, and that is enough revenge for me. Besides, people like this need to feel a little love in their lives.

For as many people who have been spiteful and nasty in this industry, there has been somebody who would take their place on the opposite side of the spectrum.

As we hosted the Festival of Dreams over a three-year period, it was common for psychics interstate or internationally to come to stay with us at our home. Ross and I, with our Mediterranean backgrounds, love hosting and feeding people, so it was no effort on our end to do so. In fact, it is something we both love to do. During the festival another one of our psychic exhibitors had spent thousands of dollars on PR publicity in order to build their business and their brand. I was horrified when our guest woke us up early on a Friday morning because his conversation with his friend who was managing a popular TV station was getting quite heated on the loudspeaker. Let's just put it this way, if you don't want someone to steal your thunder, ring a mate and make it not happen. This is exactly what our guest had done, and our exhibitor lost well over $10,000 in the process. It was a very sad outcome, but as they say, it is not always what you know it is who you know.

I couldn't help myself and told our guest that if he didn't fess up to what he had done, I would, which I found myself doing later that day. I came out of all of this as the bad guy, yet I felt so much better within myself for standing in the truth and doing what was right. You see, I don't believe in mucking around with people's livelihoods. The world has enough for all of us to share, and spite and jealousy can bring some of the greatest people down to a place their ego started from in the first place.

Our guest left our home that day, and we never saw them again. Maybe because we removed them from our festival schedule could have had something to do with it.

Dianne and I met through mutual friends, and she came to work with us not long after that. A true romantic and believer in healing and manifesting, Dianne was one of those diamonds who helped me fix my crown when it wobbled off my head. Her work is beyond amazing, and she truly lives by what she preaches. The physical distance between us never kept us apart, and she was able to see something in me that I could not see myself. Dianne is one of the people you call the 'real deal,' 'the good egg,' and someone who takes her work seriously and ethically. She would always question her readings, but I knew just by looking at her that she had the gift. Her readings became smooth and more accurate as her confidence grew.

Dianne is a true lightworker. She never sought fame or fortune, and her ability to feel other people's pain never went unnoticed. Her kindness gave her an aura of great proportions, and even though she wasn't worthy in the eyes of 'celebrity' psychics, she was worthy in mine, and that was all that mattered. We still get on the phone every few weeks or so to check in on each other. I love to hear the stories about her grandson and her latest healing modalities. Her softness and kindness could never be mistaken for weakness because

I had witnessed her turn into a fire-breathing dragon when people tried to take advantage of her.

Dianne's famous words were always "Roooosssiiieee" … and she would make me see how silly some of the things I would worry about really were. Like I said before, Dianne is the real deal, and I know her days will be spent healing people without her really trying. Just her presence and her energy are enough to fill an entire room with happiness and pure love.

The Festival of Dreams became a very stressful event for me by the end of three years of its inception. It had turned into something that was much bigger than any of us had foreseen, and I knew it was becoming far out of my league. How we turned it into something so amazing is still something I need to pinch myself over, but I can't take all of the credit. I had a good team, and Dianne was the backbone of it.

Because the Festival of Dreams became an international success, it seemed that everybody in the psychic spiritual world wanted to be my friend. I became someone who could give them something, but woe betide if I asked for something in return. Sometimes when I would find myself in a predicament that I couldn't get myself out of, Dianne was always there to hold my hand. She became my voice of reason, and every time I heard "Roooosssiiieee" I knew I was in trouble. I guess Dianne taught me one big thing about my industry: that no matter how talented, famous, or cool a psychic thought they were, it was how they treated other people that ultimately told us a lot about their integrity and personality.

Dianne and I would talk for hours on end about some of the crazy situations we had to deal with over the three-year period and some of the most amazing ones and fun ones too. I was having big problems with some of the psychics who couldn't get their shit together no matter how hard they tried, but certainly had the gift of the gab to tell others how to get their shit and lives in order. Psychics who didn't want to sit near another reader because they believed their energy was too much for the other psychic to bear, or because the other reader was putting an evil eye or a hex on them. Psychics who were not busy at our event and yet went on to blame me and the rest of my amazing team because they believed their fame and popularity made it our job to have people lining up to see them. Meanwhile, these very same psychics did not do anything to promote themselves over the weekend and sat there like big miserable lumps, who instead created rumours that we had cursed their working space so they wouldn't be busy. Absurd thinking like that can only come from insecure, fragile egos who truly believe that the world owes them something. There is an old Arabic proverb that goes like this "Trust in God but still tie up your camel." What this means is to have trust in a higher power to bring you what you need, but ultimately, don't forget it is *you* who has to do the work. It was because of Dianne during this time that I was kept sane.

It didn't help that these very psychics were charging exuberant fees for people to sit with them for just ten minutes. You barely get a "Hello, how are you?" in ten minutes, but the plan is to reel the paying client in so they will want to pay for another ten minutes, and then another ten minutes on top of that! It's a great scheme to earn a lot of money in a short time, especially if you were in the business of selling cars, but when you are a 'spiritual' psychic, it is a dirty, low, and disgusting way to earn that money.

I clearly remember feeling really bad for Lawrence, a well-known psychic within the clique. He sat there at his cubicle with a drawn-out look on his face and giving the impression that he was extremely bored. I came up to his booth to cheer him a little. He complained to me that he wasn't busy. I, being me, said as innocently as possible, "I don't understand why you aren't busy because all the other psychics are." In no way was that ever meant to be an insult to Lawrence. My delivery was taken in the wrong context. All I was really trying to say is that I couldn't understand why he, out of all the other readers, was not busy because he should have been, considering he had the best profile of the lot. In fact, I was trying to give him a compliment. I walked off, not thinking anything of it until a week after the festival. I woke up one morning, pulling the knives out of my back. Horrible things on Facebook were said about me and the festival. They were vile, vulgar, and completely false. You see, the problem with rumours is that you may offend someone unintentionally, and in your heart, you know the truth, but all the other people who were misled, deceived, and blindsided and those who started to believe the bullshit that was being said really don't.

Within weeks the rumours that I had upset Lawrence were out there, and how dare anyone upset the king of the psychic jungle! His ego was much bigger than his reputation, and his readings quite frankly were vague and wishy-washy, so much so that I actually felt bad for people who were paying money for them. Dianne had heard the gossip, and she called me to see if I was okay. Dianne also knew that I would have never intended to upset anyone, but my delivery, considering the circumstances, had been misinterpreted. I will always remember Dianne's words as she said this, "Honey, jealousy makes people tell the worst lies about you. Fake people hate honesty, and it's his lies that are making him feel good about himself."

I knew Dianne was trying to cheer me up, and I also knew that she was the first to rise to my defence. Psychics gathered in malicious gossip can be a dangerous thing, and I became their bait. What they didn't realise is that I was much stronger than all of them put together, the same reason I am still here to tell the story. This is not said in a conceited way; it is the truth. I have done the work, and I was protected. I also learnt from the best of the best, having Helen as my fairy godmother, Colin my protector, Janine, my white witch, and now Dianne, my Jiminy Cricket.

One thing that came from this experience is that it made me think about young schoolgirls and how they must feel when they are being bullied by the queen bee and her entourage in the schoolyard. If it could hurt a woman my age, I can't imagine how a child would feel. I lost some 'sisters' after that event; I was deleted and blocked on social media once again, but it also made me realise who my true friends in this business were, and I can tell you by this stage, there weren't many.

Then along came Sharina. Your faith can only keep you strong for so long, but to have special lightworkers in your camp helps to give you added strength. Lawrence had his business partner arrange his stage performance to be at the time and day he wanted. I didn't argue, I just did what I was asked and that was to give him a specific timeslot on stage. Not many people came to watch him on stage, and yet all hell broke loose when Sharina's gig at 3 pm was so busy that it packed out the whole auditorium until there was just nowhere left to stand. Lawrence went on a rampage, and with that, as well as a spoilt brat performance that could have won him an Oscar, I never saw him again. It did come back to me through the grapevine, however, that after the festival,

Lawrence was complaining that he was given the 'crumbs' on stage and was made to take the worst timeslot. I couldn't bother explaining myself. I had his emails and his partner's emails asking for that time slot; I just didn't have the energy to explain myself anymore.

It didn't take long for the gossip to get back to Sharina Star. She not only upstaged Lawrence, she also made her gig fun, light-hearted and extremely enjoyable. I will never forget a text message she sent me a few days after the event "Darl, I am going to tell you this only once – everybody isn't your friend in this industry. You are going to need some tough skin if you want to make it through alive. Just because they are in the same circle and are around you a lot does not mean that they are there for you. Psychics know how to pretend, and jealousy does not live far from their backyards. So, know who is in your circle, and at the end of the day, real situations will expose all the fake friends out there, so pay a lot of attention. Jealousy is a curse just be aware of that." It was in her words I realised that too many people spend their time hating and being jealous in a business that is coming from light. How ironic!

Coming from Sharina, her words sunk in deep. She was a veteran of the TV and media world as well as the psychic industry. I mean, a person doesn't spend twenty-seven years on TV and radio and still hangs in there for nothing. She compared the psychic world to the world of theatre, and together, we found ourselves laughing at not only the fakes but the fake acting that was accompanying it as well.

Sharina was always good for a pick me up and a good laugh and she always believed that a glass of champagne could fix anything. We would stay up chatting so many nights, and it was nice to have found solace in someone who had been around for a long while but also knew how to face the crap head-on. Lord knows, Sharina had been through her fair share of it and came out much stronger and gifted than all of them put together.

One thing Sharina said to me that always stuck in my mind was that any friend who has turned into an enemy in this industry has, in all likelihood, been jealous and hating since day one. Sharina knew as she had to work with them too, but she never gave a damn or batted an eyelid. Over the years, she has helped me to do the same.

Years on, Lawrence hadn't forgotten that weekend when his ego was shattered, and he was forced to face his worst fears, that perhaps maybe he was one of the biggest fakes in our industry. We were at a psychic event, and unbeknownst to me, we were also being filmed for a TV program. During the night, I sat with Sharina and 'our' crowd, and in fine Sharina form, she had us in fits of laughter over way too many champagnes. A completely harmless and humorous joke was made about the joys of motherhood, and as all mothers out there know, motherhood isn't always so joyous, especially if you gave birth to twins like I had. So, with that comment, I did my famous eye roll, and our table burst into more laughter. So much attention was given to our group that everyone in the room stopped to see what the commotion was all about as Sharina and I grabbed each other's hands so we wouldn't fall off our seats.

According to Lawrence, I was being extremely disrespectful that night because I had been laughing at him. If he really was a true psychic, he would have known the truth behind our laughter. Like Colin would always say, "Those who know, know and those who don't, don't," and I found myself adapting to his phrase each day as my 'spiritual' world turned into the next.

Several months later, Sharina telephoned me since I was now a regular guest on her Sunday night radio programs, and we needed to discuss our topic. During this six-minute time slot, I gave the listeners a spell of the week, along with all the Embrace gossip of the week. In our phone conversations, Sharina and I would always catch up on the latest gossip. This involved harmless topics. It was then Sharina had mentioned that the word in the psychic channel was that I was rolling my eyes in disgust at Lawrence receiving a psychic award.

Sharina knew the truth, my husband Ross also knew it, and those who were close in my circle all stood up to the rumours without me having to tell them the actual circumstances. I no longer needed to explain myself. I found myself having no reaction to this, and it was at that moment in time that I knew I was passing my wizardry exams. It was at this moment that Colin finally upgraded me from an F minus to a D.

Unlike Colin, whose words were always powerful yet serious, Sharina had this knack for saying her words powerfully but always with a comical tone. We both laughed for a long time, knowing the truth about my eye roll, and believe me, giving birth to twins definitely deserves some eye rolls!

Chapter 9

The Wolves in Sheep's Clothing

"Be careful who you trust… the devil was once an angel."

- Unknown

Did you know that two of the most powerful psychics in history were Adolf Hitler and Alastair Crowley? A bit of a shock, huh?

What if I were to tell you that not everyone gifted with psychic powers uses them for good? If Adolf and Alastair used theirs for evil, then it would only make sense that others would too.

These two men used their magic for evil, and their power came from the dark side. You see, the dark likes anything to do with sex, drugs and rock'n'roll, and even though I am not sure if rock'n'roll was around in their era, I do know that sex and drugs definitely were.

Hitler was obsessed with black magic, Satanism and psychics. He even had his very own charlatan clairvoyant by the name of Erik Jan Hanussen, an Austrian who tricked Hitler into believing he was German. Hanussen rose to fame and fortune in the 1920s, and his wealth and fame as a psychic, mentalist and hypnotist eventually led him to a violent death once Hitler had found out the truth of his Jewish origins. It's an interesting story, and I urge you to look more into it yourself. Let's face it, if someone as evil and sinister as Hitler could be fooled, then the rest of us would have no hope.

Crowley, the eccentric occultist of the early 20th century, used a multi-layered template of magical systems which incorporated the Kabbalah, meditation, sexual rituals, excessive drug use and a great deal more. He was dubbed "the wickedest man in the world," and yet, many occultists and spiritualists just love and adore his work.

Colin would always say to me, "Not everything is as it seems." He would always talk to me in riddles and leave me to work out the answer. And so, over the 30 something years, I look back at the Hitlers and Alistairs I actually worked with, who are now still giving psychic readings, still playing with people's heads, and still earning more money than some of the hardest working professionals I have ever known. It seems to me that the more famous a psychic can make their work seem, the more valuable it becomes when you are given an eye-watering price tag, and no one bats an eyelid! By doing this, it allows their teachings to seem more valuable in the marketplace. Being on TV, collecting certificates and being a celebrity psychic is like using pseudo-science, psychology, spirituality, and a feel-good message as bait. It is a very clever marketing device with very subtle deception. Not all psychics with certificates, who are on TV or who have read for celebrities fall into this category though, but I can assure you that they are few and far between.

For a die-hard psychic junkie or a regular client, there comes a time when they have to ask themselves where exactly do these psychics get their information from? For me, all I can say is it is a knowing. A deep in your belly kind of feeling you get when the truth has just set you free. I am a seer; I can see, I can also hear, and I can also feel. Being an empath is a blessing and a curse all rolled into one. I will never open myself up for a reading without thorough protection. I say the Lord's Prayer before any work I delve into. I bring down the white light. I protect myself energetically, and I prepare my mind, body and spirit. I will never go into a reading fully open and without protection, as I could never guarantee where my information will be channelled from. I am the biggest scaredy-cat when it comes to the Ouija board as I am totally aware of the portals and energy it can attract. I will not play with this sort of energy, and I refuse to sell them at Embrace. By no means am I saying that people who work with the Ouija are bad people, as I have many close friends, including Janine, who work with it properly. It is when it gets into the wrong hands that things can go all pear-shaped.

I cannot even begin to tell you how many teenage girls come into Embrace wanting to buy an Ouija board and how many lectures I find myself giving them about it. I blame a lot of the teenage shows like Charmed, for example, who make this sort of thing really cool when it is far from it.

When people are open and play with the dark side, all hell can break loose, and they have no idea what it is they are actually playing with. Needless to say, it's a game they will never win. So, it is energetically important to prepare yourself to receive messages from the light and only the light. It takes a lot to get there, but all you need is a kind heart, a gentle soul, and a strong belief in the Higher Power.

In many of my talks and seminars, I have spoken about the astral plane. I never understood the Catholic meaning of purgatory, but I guess the astral is something like that, and something like the train station scene in the movie, 'Ghost.' Patrick Swayze plays the role of Sam, who finds himself at a train station in Manhattan where there are endless amounts of ghosts, all hanging around in limbo who had missed the light to go home. I guess you can say these ghosts are bored and have nothing else to do, so they like to play tricks on people and entertain themselves in their own kind of freaky way. Trust me when I say, as a psychic, this is not the place you want to be getting your messages from, yet unfortunately, it is the most common place most psychics do get their information from.

How many times over the years have I been the first-hand witness to psychics at Embrace running in late, scoffing down the last bit of their chocolate muffin and extra shot latte whilst busting to go to the bathroom, holding it in, and quickly dashing the tarot cards out of their bag and go straight headbang into their reading. Seriously? What do you think is the most likely thing that is going to happen here? Of course, a lot of these mischievous spirits are already in the psychic's energy field and start to have a lot of fun at the psychic's and client's expense. Oh, you may just find that these naughty spirits might like to go home with the client, and the rest is predictable! How many times had I needed to close down portals when psychics left them open after a busy day or console clients because strange things were going bump in the night after their reading that day. I can't even count how many times Embrace was left with stuck heavy energy because the psychic hadn't bothered to clean themselves before the reading the way a surgeon would before his surgery.

People always ask me why I am the fussiest and most sceptical person out there when it comes to psychics. I can answer steadfastly as I have worked with some of the best of the best, and some of the worst of the worst, and some of the in-betweens. If I do not know where the psychic is getting their information from, then they don't read for me, and they definitely no longer work at Embrace, either in store or via our online bookings. At one stage, we had many readers working for us, and now I have brought it down to only a hand-selected few and I prefer it that way.

It's a scary world out there sometimes, but it is even scarier when you are amongst the world of the astral. It is not a place where I want to be and not a place where you would want to be either. I can guarantee you that you will be hooked if your psychic is reading from that place, but I also can bet your bottom dollar that this is where all your future trouble will lay.

Don't be fooled by exhibitions or events that you may attend that are all in the name of spirituality, health, wellness, and the likes. You must remember that the organisers of these events are running them to create a business for themselves and therefore they are run as one. This also included my very own Festival of Dreams. It was first and foremost a business with a great business model, and secondly, it was a spiritual event. I am not taking away from anyone running the business, but when I walk into these fairs and find not-so-nice people pretending to be something they are not, I have to take a deep breath.

I have a very good friend who I have known for years. She is an extremely educated and well-spoken woman with a sharp wit and an observing mind. Her achievements run long, and her walls are filled with university degree after university degree. She has never known what it feels like to achieve anything other than a high distinction. I recall many years ago a phone call I received from her in desperation and asking me to come over as a matter of urgency. She had found out that her partner of nine years had been molesting her young children, and she did not hesitate to call the police. As he slept in a prison cell the night she disclosed all his crimes to me, she was beside herself with anxiety and worry. Her children came first, and that was that. I commended the way she put them first and was able to get this man out of her life without hesitation. Some other girlfriends and I took it in turns to help with the cooking and child-minding whilst Suzy worked, and we were all there for her during this hideous man's court trial.

You can only imagine my surprise when I was walking through an ever-busy spiritual festival, and lo and behold saw this paedophile working amongst some Buddhist monks healing unsuspecting participants as they walked by the booth he was working from. Nobody in that room that day had any idea that he was on parole except for me. The wonderful Buddhist monks who have such an amazing message to tell would have been mortified if they had known the truth about one of their "healers." It took every bit of courage not to yell out abuse to this man, and instead, I walked the corner and threw up. From my understanding, he is still in a jail cell to this day, but my point is that we never really know who somebody really is. Just because somebody is working at a business level at an event like this does not necessarily make them a spiritual being.

I am so passionate about this subject that I urge anyone reading this book to really take note. I would not be where I am today if it wasn't for the light, the real lightworkers I work with, and the knowledge that has been passed to me from my teachers and those I call the 'real deal.' There are truly so many honest, ethical, and really good people in our industry, it is just a matter of using strong discernment to find them. Honestly, thirty years in this industry is enough to write at least ten books on the subject, but that would take me a lifetime, and I don't have that much time left to spread my message.

When Melody walked into Embrace one day with a much older man who I thought was her father (who actually wasn't, but instead was somebody else's husband), I could see straight away that she had a gift. After I questioned her about it, she confirmed in the affirmative, and she began to read at Embrace the following week. At first, I thought she was brilliant, but I failed to recognise that she was not using her talents for the good of all concerned. Purely nasty in nature, I didn't take any notice of it until it was too late. Perhaps I didn't want to believe it when everyone around me could see it, but also because she filled in a gap at the shop that I so badly needed to be filled. Clients loved her, and yet there was something curiously strange. She had this way of being able to pierce your soul and have you wondering where it went. She was charming, beautiful, talented, and downright pure evil. Yes, the devil sometimes does wear Prada. I will always remember my dear friend Yvonne point out Melody's feet and tell me she had Reptilian blood as there was almost a web-like look about them. I would laugh poor Vonnie off and think nothing more until the day I was left with no other choice than to fire her.

We take great pride in keeping Embrace clean and vibrant energetically. It only took one woman to walk in there and turn that energy into complete darkness and chaos.

Seductively and secretly, she was like poison ivy that came in small and went out big. I was going home with massive headaches; I was tired and started to get sick a lot. My staff were vomiting on the job for no reason, and the shop started to feel very dark and murky. The trained eye could see it, and I was beside myself. Short-staffed, busy, a single mother of baby twins, I was desperate to find a way out of the jungle I found Embrace in. It felt like the shop had been raped by a vicious, callous, calculating, and narcissistic soul who couldn't bear to be in Embrace's light, so they dimmed it down until all the staff started to quarrel, and the readers were a different personality each day, depending on whatever the weather was, or the moon, or mercury retrograde, or whatever else they liked to blame it on. Our busiest psychic was no longer getting readings, our phone line, which never stops, did stop, and things started to feel eerie.

I felt like I was in a murky swamp, sinking deeper into the quicksand, and had only one lifeline to save me. I called in Janine.

Melody would come into Embrace admitting that she had no sleep the night before as she would have demons and entities attacking her all night. When I suggested she perhaps cleanse herself before her readings, she looked at me as if I had no idea what I was talking about. I find it interesting as I write this that the day Melody came to work for us, our shop became infested with cockroaches. No matter how much spray or pest control we did, we could not get rid of them. The day she left is the day the cockroaches made their exit also, and we never ever saw another one since.

Together Janine and I did some energy work on the shop, and along with our witchy partner Effie, the power of three could still not overshadow the power we were dealing with. One by one, my psychics started turning on each other, bitching, moaning, backstabbing, and nastiness are the only words I can think of as I pull these memories out of a deep dark hole I sank them into. It has been said many times before that it only takes one rotten tomato to ruin the bunch, and as each psychic turned on each other, I found myself becoming depressed and sad.

For the first time ever, my psychics began questioning me about their pay. Not only were a small handful of psychics stealing from me in stock, but they started to steal clients also. Like any other who came from the dark, Melody believed it was her duty to create utter chaos and madness in a place that was going along so smoothly without her. I had no one else to blame but myself, and once I realised that, I knew it was time to do something drastic.

Melody's biggest mistake was trusting other psychics with her secrets. Just as you wouldn't tell your hairdresser what you don't want the world to know, so too, you have to be very selective as to what psychic you choose to disclose your deeper, inner confidential thoughts to. Melody loved nothing more than to come out of her readings and tell whoever wanted to listen about her client's affairs, and it became evident that when I pulled her up on this, she wanted to take her revenge. Melody cornered all the readers individually and tempted them the same way Eve tempted Adam (even though we all know Eve was framed by the serpent). Melody started to lead my psychics and my staff to her poison, and only a few survived.

With her sweet, quiet voice, Melody talked to them one on one with the promises of not telling a soul, except she told the next soul in order to turn the readers upon each other. The gossip became more vicious, and the shop became a playground of cockroaches and gossip. The only way I can truly describe this is to imagine that they were all on a drug, wandering around aimlessly and being enchanted under her hypnotic charm.

After causing the chaos of the century with our readers, Melody thought it would be fun to create the same sort of trouble with my staff. Mind you, this time, she used their boyfriends to play with as her bait. And this is where it all got too interesting and too complicated. I found myself being like a school principal, having to pull everyone back in line. However, Melody took her final bow when, in the midst of a staff meeting, she very casually spoke up to tell us how she would masturbate over her clients straight after their reading was finished. I think my mouth must have dropped open for more than a minute as it had nowhere else to go, but wide in shock. I found myself shaking my head and answering her with a "What?" Not only did she have her own fun with her clients, she then went on to tell us how she would fantasise about Celina and I having a threesome with her. This time my mouth stayed open, and I was shaking. Melody's eyes turned into elliptical ones, and I just looked into her serpent eyes and said, "Leave." To tell you I used every bit of sage that was in the shop is not an overstatement.

I saged, I incensed, I disinfected and prayed like a crazy woman who desperately needed to get her dirty house back into some sort of decent clean order. Janine and Effie helped energetically get our baby back to where it was, and this time, the power of three became an almighty warrior.

Melody, with no teaching experience, absolutely no people skills, or any concept of what happens when you deal with the dark, ended up in a psychiatric ward sometime after. The Shire is a small place, and knowing people who worked at the hospital who had assured me she wouldn't be out for a long while, I started to feel much safer. Many years on, Melody now charges over $600 a reading, and teaches psychic development classes at a ridiculous cost. In between that, she still frequents the psychiatric home because voodoo and dark magic just don't mix well. Her clients are still the same, being caught in her spider web with no way out, yet her readings are good because she knows how to find the hook, and butter wouldn't melt in her mouth, along with the handsome cash bundle she kept under her mattress. That is, until the day the taxman came looking for her.

I picked Renae up from the airport and insisted she stay at our home to save herself money on renting a hotel for the next few days whilst she was in Sydney teaching a psychic development workshop. Her three-day event consisted of modules where the students had to learn to keep energetically clean, which also translates into keeping themselves hygienically clean. After three days of sleeping at my home, Renae had not once taken a shower. I ensured that she had clean towels when she arrived, and the very same towels came back to me the way they were when they went from my arms into hers. She didn't even brush her teeth, and yet she stood tall in all her glory in front of her class and gave them the workshop of a lifetime as she discussed every single hygiene practice you can do to keep yourself safe from psychic attacks and dark energies. Charging her classes out at $400 a pop with ten students in the class, it wasn't a bad income for three days' work. I'm not sure about you, but I sure as hell know that I want to get what I had paid for and to feel assured that my teacher is not only the right deal but also someone who practices what she preaches.

Then came along Bob. When he found out that I was doing a festival, he so badly wanted to be a part of it, and he graciously offered to help in any way he could.

Unbeknownst to me, however, I didn't realise that his way of helping was actually to take over the whole event.

I knew how much it meant to him to be involved as he was moving into his late sixties and worrying about his ever-increasing health problems and concerned that he would not be around to make it another year. Mind you, this was eleven years ago, and Bob is still around, fit enough to tell the story plus moreover many years to come. I didn't really have a lot for Bob to help me with, but I explained to him on the morning of the opening how important it was to me to have an opening prayer and welcome to the country meditation session. Because it was my gig, I obviously wanted to hold this myself, and I asked Bob if he would gather the people involved around so we could get the meditation started. As he was doing so, I walked back into my store to grab some water. I walked out to see Bob starting the meditation and opening ceremony without me. I stood there, blinked my eyes about a hundred times whilst shaking my head and mouthing WTF?

I was more shocked at how rude he was to start something so sacred without involving me, the host, and having the audacity to take over the whole event. I don't think I cried as much as I had that day, and in true typical psychic fashion, the moment I had a word with him about it, I became the bad guy. How dare I upset Bob with all his health conditions, how rude I was not to respect that he had been working as a psychic for the past 50 years, how inconsiderate that I was upset he took over my event, the one I created and orchestrated from conception to end and spent 1000s of dollars on from my own pocket. Ten years on, Bob puts his head down in shame whenever he sees me at psychic events. I got over it, but I never got an apology. I wasn't really expecting one, but I wasn't expecting the backlash I received either from his circle of friends for many weeks and years after the event.

Bob became another snake in the grass I had to watch out for and sadly one of many. He is still out there, giving readings and pretending to be somebody he is not, and people love him. They just don't realise that he has to take off his disguise every night before going to bed.

Another psychic I had the non-pleasure of working with was Becky. One week she would come to work as a straight woman; the following, she was gay. The following week after that, she was bi, and then the week following that one, she wasn't sure if she was Arthur or Martha. Do not get me wrong, I have no judgment on her sexual preference or gender, but what I do hold against her is her involvement and the advice she gave to her clients. A sex addict by nature, Becky was able to find the most vulnerable clients and show them the love she thought they deserved. In the name of "spirituality," she offered her sexual services for free to her clients in return for them becoming more sexually free as she believed it would be more liberating for them. So free, in fact, that I witnessed quite a few women leaving their husbands, their children, and their family lives behind to explore their sexuality, losing everything they had ever known so precious to them. Some, and mind you, a very few, went on to have amazing lives with no regrets, but they were few and far between the destruction and chaos Becky was creating for not only the client but their families as well.

Not formally trained in any sort of counselling, Becky is still out there doing the same to many more unsuspecting victims. I find that very sad. It was a known fact within the industry that Becky was having an affair with another well-known psychic. Again, no judgment on my end, but my problem was when she felt it necessary to give unprofessional and really bad advice to men and women who were doing the same thing. With no rules or regulations in the industry, anyone and everyone is fair game, and the rules can be played any way the psychic likes. At least with a trained counsellor they do not tell you what to do, and instead, help you make that decision yourself.

I guess you can say the psychic "groomers" have to be up there with the worst of the worst in our industry. I already told you about the healer that can make women orgasm over computer zoom sessions in order to help clear out their base chakras, but I didn't tell you about the other healers who feel it is their duty to take away a young girl's innocence all in the name of "shamanism." That way, they can plant their energetic seed and brainwash their client into believing something they call universal love. What it really is, is a dirty old man who can get his rocks off over yet another vulnerable and unsuspecting victim (oops, I meant client) and get them to believe it is love when it is just a way for the dirty old man to get his rocks off. No more, no less. Just take a look at John of God, and I rest my case.

We had a guest psychic come into Embrace for a day as a fun thing for our customers. She lived quite far away, and she had already gained herself a small handful of fans who had seen her in the public field. She strutted into our shop, and I ushered her to the room she would be using for the day. With that, she pulled out wads, and I mean like the wads you would see in movies, with drug dealers' type of cash wads. The cash was falling to the floor as she didn't have it secured, and she started smelling it and holding it out for me to smell.

I sort of just stood there thinking how bizarre. She must have sensed my uneasiness and told me that she had more of that at home as she had just secured herself a psychic gig that was paying her a few thousand a night, all cash in hand. I thought for a moment that maybe I was in the wrong end of the psychic field, but I heard the taxman eventually got a hold of her. I realise that I am quite comfortable where I am right now, and I am able to sleep quite comfortably at night. The taxman is someone I really didn't want to play with, but I suppose karma does eventually catch up with you in the end.

I have to tell you the story about a psychic, Andrew, and his wife, Celestine. God forgive me for saying this, but these guys came along in my early Embrace years, and boy, had I not met a bigger pair of whingers and whiners in my whole life. Do you know the couple that you see in the movies that everyone tries to avoid? Well, sadly for Andrew and Celestine, they were that couple. They never had any money between them, and they made it quite clear to make sure everybody knew about it. Scammers at best, where ever these guys went, they managed to get free breakfasts, lunches, and dinners at the expense of the poor unsuspecting clients they had just read for. True gypsies making a home where ever they travelled until they ran their luck with the locals and moved onto the next town. Along with many other psychics in the industry I know, I was also fooled into believing the poor me mentality and lost a bit of cash along the way in what I believed was a good deed for the day.

These guys loved good gossip, and they then loved nothing more to make sure the whole world knew about the gossip, but this time, it came from the mouth of whoever it was they were telling the story to. Needless to say, these two didn't make many friends in the industry as they not only backstabbed their way through it, they were dishonest and unscrupulous. Together they practiced black magic, and even though I don't believe in spells and curses, I really don't like the thought that someone is trying to do that to me anyway. I could never understand a word they said as they both spoke so fast. I chuckle to think that perhaps their spells weren't working because whoever it was on the other side making spells work, probably couldn't understand a word they were saying either!

I can honestly say I was happy to see the end of these two, but I do wonder about them from time to time, and wonder where in the world they are, and who they are pulling the same old trick on.

You know how in the movies, there always seems to be that group of kids who are the bullies in the playground? That is what my work sometimes feels like where I am the headmaster, as they all enter my office one by one, telling on each other.

Five years after Taryn and I worked at a psychic event together, she was introduced through a mutual friend. I was pleasant yet a bit standoffish. She assured me what a great reader she was, and it is really not that very hard to tell when someone is faking his or her way to success and believing in the lies they tell. I know that if a person repeats a lie often enough, it becomes the truth for them. You would expect this sort of behaviour in politicians, car salesmen and shonky snake oil dealers, not from people who claim to be from the light and preaching spirituality like it was the coolest thing to do. I only met Taryn a few times, and even though she asked if she could come work as a reader at Embrace, I politely declined because we were already full.

I am glad I followed my intuition because as quickly as Taryn had come into my life for that brief moment, and I had forgotten all about her, she came back with a vengeance many years later. She took my decline in having her work at Embrace as an insult, but I had to follow my gut with this one, and I did what I believed was best for my shop. It is always in times like these that I am so grateful that I listen to my gut. You see, years had gone past, 5 to be exact, when Taryn decided to make an anonymous call to Embrace. My poor 16-year-old junior picked up the phone to cop the brunt of Taryn's anger and demanded to speak with me. I was not there, so Taryn hung up. The following day, the same thing happened, but this time she left a message for me to call. I was so busy that I honestly forgot to call her back, not even realising that it was the woman I had worked with at the psychic fair all those years before.

By the third day, she called again and this time, she was abusing my staff and blaming me because she apparently had a brain tumour. Apparently, I had energetically planted it that day, five years prior, at the psychic event we met at. I am not really sure why I chose her to implant a tumour, but apparently, I did. Spirit had told her that I was also involved in the mafia, and I was the leader of a huge drug cartel coming in from Brazil. I can assure you that the only things I had coming into Embrace from Brazil were amethyst crystals, and with that, I had to laugh. Not that she had a brain tumour, or did she? But the Spirit she was talking to was definitely not the Spirit that I talk to. I am not sure what happened with her health, but I do wonder why she chose me, someone she had known for all but 5 minutes, to target.

My adopted grandmother Helen told me to leave the monkey alone and not entertain it. Still, the inquisitive cat in me became so curious about what this woman was on about that I started to do some investigating on my own. Sure enough, Taryn had been placed into a psychiatric ward with severe paranoid schizophrenia, which she was born with. I tell you of this story because as a client, you really must be careful who you get your readings from as we really have no idea what goes on behind closed doors.

Corey was a customer I met in Embrace in its early days. When I say he was handsome, I mean so handsome that you just couldn't take your eyes off him. His face was perfect, his eyes blue, and he had that whole puppy dog look happening the way Hugh Grant pulls off in Bridget Jones' Diary. Corey was shy, and I was always in quite a shock when he told me that he had no idea how to find himself a girlfriend. He was definitely great to look at but to talk to was a whole new ball game. His conversations were awkward, and he was very shy. I knew at the time that Corey was studying massage, and he was right into the whole reiki thing and wanting to use Embrace as a stepping stone to get his healing career off the ground.

Unfortunately for Corey, I had no space for him. I let him know that as soon as I did, I would definitely let him know. I never heard from him again, but I had a dream of him eight years later, which made me so inquisitive as to why I had to search him up and stalk his Facebook page. There was this shy, quiet, awkward man who is now a high-paying massage therapist and teaches women how to have a good time. You see, it's not only men who can have happy endings after their massage, and Corey found a loophole with his good looks and massage skills to finally hook in the ladies.

His marketing ploy was strategically clever, and even though he was nothing more than a high-paid escort, he paraded himself as a healer for women who needed to be healed. He marketed hymen massage as a way to help women relax and open up (pun intended), and lessons in bondage and boudoir photos as a way to show women how sexy they could really be. To this day, I can't help but admire his marketing skills and his nous for even giving it a go, but I will never understand the women who could fall for it all.

Apparently, Corey has a thriving business, and you know what, good on him. I just hope that women don't misinterpret healing and sex as one and the same. He offered me a massage, and I politely declined and went home to my home-cooked meal, fighting kids and doting husband. Corey is still healing the socks of the ladies, drives around in a red Lamborghini, and his now grey hair has given him even a more handsome look. Just be careful is all I can say, and perhaps become friends with Jessica Rabbit instead! At least she can sit at your bedside table, and you will only have to pay once for her!

Back in the early days when I started my career as a psychic and began to work in the crystal shops, we had a manager who was much older than us maidens. When you are in your twenty-somethings, and someone is in their forty-somethings, you tend to see them as quite old. Well, we did anyway. I had a very uneasy feeling whenever I was around the manager who didn't happen to be in the shop much, but when she was, it was an awkward feel. I would always sense her probing into my psyche as if she was trying to read my mind, and in defence I would automatically put my shield up so she couldn't pry through. Needless to say, our manager didn't like me doing this, and so she and I had this sort of power play going on. There were times I felt I needed to search the store for some kryptonite as her energy was so powerful that it would literally knock me into a dizzy head spin, and her hidden stash of kryptonite was weakening me.

Every month our manager held a staff meeting at her home with the staff, and I was expecting an actual staff meeting when I got there. It was a really windy and rainy night, and even though the air was muggy, I was extremely overdressed in too many layers of warm clothes. Once inside, I removed my jacket, and our manager straight away said that I will be removing many more of my clothes before the night was out. I didn't think much of her comment, assuming she had the heat on high. When I tell you, it got hot in there, I am not exaggerating! The meeting went for a short twenty minutes, and within seconds of it concluding, we were asked who wanted to stay behind to have some fun. At first thought, I assumed the fun she was referring to was smoking a joint, but I was far removed from reality when one of my teammates told me that was our cue to join in on an orgy.

I still clearly remember that night as a massive loud bang of thunder came rumbling through the room the moment she said the word "orgy." Asking her to repeat herself in order to make sure the thunder hadn't deafened what I thought I had heard, I then found myself giggling. Our manager asked me what I thought was so funny and with that, I said the words "You! I find you funny," and I never went back to work for her again.

A few of the girls stayed back that night, and they were the same girls who always got the extra bonuses each week in their pay and the same girls who believed that their manager was some sort of guru and for that she must be rewarded.

It wasn't until a year later, at a well-established spiritual fair, that I saw the manager on the stage speaking about love. I looked around at her captivated audience, and as I walked away halfway through her talk, I found myself thinking out loud that one day I will write a book about all of this and expose the whole damn lot of 'em!

I feel the best way to finish this chapter is with a quote from the Bible that Colin would always repeat to me: "Beware of false prophets, who come to you in sheep's clothing but inwardly are ravenous wolves." - Matthew 7:15

Chapter 10

Psychos in the Suburbs, on TV and Everywhere Else You Look

"Life is about finding the kind of people who are your kind of crazy."

- Unknown

I heard a quote once that only psychos and shamans create their own reality. It took me some time to fully grasp the true meaning behind it until I actually started working with both psychos and shamans and let's throw a few psychics in there as well.

Let me take you on a journey down memory lane, a memory I would rather forget but one that has me sitting back and thinking that perhaps this book should become a blockbuster movie!

It was sometime in the '90s when Maxine came into my reading room for me to tell her everything that she wanted to hear. I did. But not because she wanted me to, but because that was where her cards were laying at the time.

Week after week, she came back for more until she was seeing up to three psychics a day! In our world, we call a person like this a psychic junkie. The person I was working for at the time told me that under no circumstances was I to ever refuse her a reading no matter what my conscience or integrity told me. Maxine was a great financial asset to the company until I could no longer be a part of the lack of ethics this establishment held. I broke the news to Maxine gently that I would be leaving. Even though she pleaded for my phone number, I knew in my heart that it was not the right thing to do, to steal a client from another business and also to keep her relying on a psychic when she needed to learn how to rely on herself.

A few years older than me, I started to hold a soft spot for Maxine. I could tell that she was very troubled and a huge part of me just wanted to wrap myself around her and tell her that everything would be OK. The problem was that Maxine liked drama, and so she found herself always in a pickle and choosing the wrong men. It was many years later when our paths crossed again, but this time, her energy had changed. Life over that time had made her even harder. It showed in each crease in her face, and her lack of trust in the world. I have found over the years that when people lack trust, it is because they are lacking trust within themselves. Maxine was no exception.

She told me about the love of her life and how they were to be married. As a psychic, every hair on my body stood up and my gut was feeling ill. There was something in her story that wasn't making sense, and, in a flash, I envisioned a narcissist womanizer who couldn't be trusted with his own mother's pair of socks! I just got a bad feeling for her and something in me knew that he was most definitely not the love of her life the way she had thought. I broke the news gently and with that, I had become the bad guy. Don't you just love it when you try to do something to help someone before they fall any deeper, and all of a sudden, you find yourself as the bad guy?

I should have known better than to get involved, but I did it anyway. As a psychic junkie, it didn't take long for word to get out that I had stolen Maxine's boyfriend. As much as she wanted to build picket fences with this guy, it wasn't going to happen. When you rely on psychics your whole life for any decision, including what to have for dinner that night (I wish I was joking), and you don't hear what you want to hear, the next logical move (said extremely sarcastically) is to become a psychic yourself! So, in that, Maxine came a psychic just the way I am going to become the next newest kid on the block on Broadway! As fate would have it, I found out that this bad guy Maxine was so madly in love with was a distant cousin! Seriously, what were the chances of all the bad guys in the world, it had to be someone who was actually related to me, albeit very distantly. I know this guy too well, and my intuition was spot on when I warned Maxine about him previously. Let's just say he was far from marriage material!

With that, and in a rage that not only had I stolen her boyfriend, I now am in a kissing cousin relationship which is why, according to Maxine, they broke up. Either way, I was never going to win with this one, so I became the subject of her next obsession, and my life as I knew it started to become an absolute turmoil. Maxine went out of her way to stand outside Embrace and warn everyone who entered that

I was her boyfriend stealer. Either she made herself look mad or made me look like a big tart, this was never going to end well. Within weeks, certain psychics could no longer work with me because of "What I did to Maxine." Other psychics were being threatened by her, that if they did not read for her, then she would commit suicide. Others, who did not work at Embrace, would insult me because "how dare" I upset Maxine so much.

Most people would get revenge (if they were inclined that way) by boiling my rabbit or running their car into me. Maxine, on the other hand, would have done both if I had a rabbit and if I actually drove, so instead, she did what any crazy bitch would do and opened a psychic shop right next to Embrace. Try to envision this if you could…you have your Catholic school girls in one area and then you have not-so-good Catholic girls in the next. And yes, just as you can imagine, a circus was formed!

A yearly spring fair happens each September in our area, where everyone from the Shire attends to celebrate the beginning of our Aussie spring. Whilst I was waiting in line to pay for the Ferris wheel my kids wanted to go on, Maxine came pushing through the crowds and faced me with vengeance in her voice and hatred in her words. She was aggressive and threatening and promised not only to have me killed but that she would be watching every move I made. With that, my children became frightened and started to cry. Just like the mother lioness protecting her cubs, I ushered my kids away from there as quickly as possible. It wasn't until later that night when I was going over the scenario in my head that I realised that it is not always possible to carry the light and that a bit of dark also shone in me.

Without the protection of Colin around me this time, I had to very quickly grow my own wings, and when she told me that I needed to watch my back because she knew where I lived, I found myself with no reaction. Later that night, I was forwarded a screenshot from a friend who had seen the crazy lady's Facebook post about how I came to the festival that day to spy on her business. Many people got in on the conversation, and some very hurtful and untrue things were said. I closed my eyes, and I prayed. There really wasn't much more that I could do.

Of course, I felt a sting, but it wasn't the crazy lady's words that hurt me; it was the responses from people who knew me, even though she never mentioned my name. These comments were from other psychics, other seers, other spiritualists, other healers and anything other than nice people. One comment from a well-known Reiki healer who practices kindness and compassion got me really hard. He is known for his softness and gentleness and his humane way of looking out for this world. He works with nature, and you can sometimes find him reading his client through a flower or plant, a quite impressive way to read. I had never met this man, in fact, we live in different states, but I had heard of him, and he had definitely heard of me. It's always a six degrees of separation thing in the psychic industry where everyone knows of everyone.

So, after the crazy lady not only attacked me in public, she then went on to attack me on social media, and in one reply, this caring, gentle peacemaker wrote back to her, "I have a gun. Would you like me to use it?"

Five years on, and I still do not have any words to describe the fear and hurt I held in my heart for a long while after that. Even if he was joking, it definitely was not a nice joke, and it absolutely is not the right thing to say or do when you practice so much love and light in your life. I have heard since then that this man has caused a lot of grief in the lives of some people who have crossed paths with him, but in the same token, he goes on to make a career "healing" lives all in the name of Reiki. As for Maxine, all the psychics she had working for her left on bad terms, and so she had no other choice than to become a psychic herself in order for her business to continue. That in itself freaked me out, considering I had first met her 20 years prior when she had come to me for a psychic reading. With not a psychic bone in her body, and a reputation of a psychic junkie (someone who cannot make any decisions in their life, including what to cook for dinner without consulting a psychic), and a history of mental illness, the crazy woman has branded herself a psychic life coach.

I was shocked when Colin told me that it was time to prepare for battle, and Helen quoted JFK and told me that the only way to secure peace was to prepare for war. Janine was teaching me how to do some heavy-duty protection and returning it all back to the sender. I was more than a little shocked as I thought my three goody two shoes would tell me to turn the other cheek or to tell me that the best revenge was to smile and move on. It was in this moment that Colin sat me down and explained to me that there was a huge difference between protecting yourself and seeking revenge.

All the good I was doing was being attacked and my three main heroes were telling me to react? I understand that every garden gets invaded but that was meant to happen in other people's gardens, not mine.

It was almost a year later when I walked past Maxine at a spiritual event and our eyes locked. I think I froze for half a second, which felt like an eternity, and in my softest voice, I said a faint hello, nodded my head, and kept on walking. By this stage, I could hear my heart beating, and Maxine's voice in the background yelled for me to stop. I turned to look back, and she had followed me from where she was to where I was, and in the softest manner, asked me why I had said hello to her. I thought it was a rather strange question to ask, and I replied because we knew each other and our eyes had just locked, so it was the polite thing to do. She then questioned why, because she thought I didn't like her, and I found myself replying that no, I actually didn't really like her much, but why should that stop me from being civil and polite and acting in a way Jesus would do by being kind. She shrugged her shoulders and walked away, and that was the end of that until thirty minutes later, my phone started to ring. "Oh my god, Rosie... what did you do to Maxine? She is at her stand crying because you just came around to bully her." In those short seconds, I felt like I wanted the floor to open up and suck me into the abyss. I asked Ross to come back with me to see her and set the record straight, and even though he thought it was a bad idea, he came back with me anyway. By this stage, Maxine had an entourage of psychics who I knew were pandering to her tears and wiping them away. One, who I thought was a friend and who should have known my personality to a T, told me point blank that it wasn't a nice thing what I did to Maxine, and the other psychics all nodded their heads in agreement.

I called on Colin, who came with us that day to the fair and who liked to always go in his own direction. He told me that there was nothing wrong with being polite to someone despite all the things we didn't agree upon, and he pulled me aside in the midst of hundreds of people and made me stare at the crowd that had now gathered around Maxine in hurtful gossip.

Colin asked me what I could see, and since I had been crying, it wasn't much. We played this game for over an hour, and I was getting frustrated and just wanted to go home, but he wasn't letting me go anywhere until I learnt to play chess even though it looked like the bad guys were winning.

So, I stared, and I stared until finally, it dawned on me. I knew exactly what Colin was trying to get me to see, and that was Maxine's tribe and their auras. They were all exactly the same! He then made me look at his and at Ross's, and I realized that theirs was the same as mine. After scanning the room for auras and matching this goes with that, it occurred to me that energy goes where energy flows. Maxine's crowd had a dark murkiness in their auric field, and even though there was a smidgen of light, it wasn't enough to break through, no matter how much these people wanted it to. It was a classic case of "birds of a feather flock together," and I got a big fat A+ from Colin as he ticked off yet again another assessment task.

I walked away that afternoon while Maxine walked the stage to present a talk on how to live a happy life by working with positive energies. I smiled and quietly thought to myself that this life really is one big stage, and we are mere mortals playing our role. I knew at that moment that I was never going to let her or any other intruder of the dark ruin all the good I had started.

Another year had passed when Maxine called Embrace and demanded a psychic reading from one of our readers. My staff were not aware it was her over the phone, and we could not fit her in on that day. With that, she threatened that she will kill herself and it would be our fault for not allowing her to see a reader. The psychics had all been totally booked that day, and we were not purposely being spiteful; we just couldn't get her a reading. It was about a week later I heard she had closed shop, and that is when she reinvented herself into a life coach. When oh when will the government enforce some sort of regulations? I'm not sure about you, but I surely wouldn't want to be coached by a crazy lady in the street who pulls on another's hair, makes threats to her children, and then threatens to kill herself if she doesn't get her own way!

For many years I had a big problem with psychic phone lines and psychic TV programs. In 2010, I had been invited to consult for a program and give them my advice on how to run their psychic show. I sat through many lunch hours with them, guiding them the best I knew how and introducing them to many other psychics I had known. I, too, had been invited to read on the show, but my blood turned sour when all the advice I had given them went right out the window, and they decided to run it their own way. That was fine, it was their show anyway, but it was the lack of integrity and ethics that had turned me away from working with these guys.

We all know what a scam is, and sadly, we all more than likely have been a victim of a scam, but when a scam is done right in front of your eyes, you would be stupid and very foolish to go along with it and to be a part of it. Am I right? A few months into consulting for these guys, it came to be that they needed to collect as many 'psychics' as they could for their programme. They were not interested in whether the psychic was really a psychic or not. To get a job on their programme, nobody needed to actually be a psychic, and their criteria was anyone who could look good on camera and who had the gift of the gab (Australian slang for talk) who could talk to people confidently about their problems. One night in their studio, I sat with the psychics before the programme aired, and I listened in horror when the producer told them all to just wing it and make up their reading while keeping it juicy and making sure the clients were kept on the phone lines for as long as possible. This way, as the minutes were ticking, the clients were being extorted, and the psychics were being paid on a bonus package depending on how many 'minutes' of clients' time they had accrued in a night.

You see, the cost of the phone call would be a set fee, and usually, the first few minutes are free, and the goal is to convert these readings into full-length readings while the clock is ticking. When the minutes are down, a lot of pressure is placed on the psychic, and they have to think of something, anything. The best hook to keep someone entertained on the line long enough is to be the bearer of bad news. It's an old trick, and it works. I mean, who would want to get off the phone after you have just been told your world is about to come crashing down or that you have an evil spell or curse on you? Think about it.

I am a businesswoman. I know and understand business, but I will be darned if I was ever to bleed dry a customer for the sake of making myself some dollars. For one, clients are paying for a service with a psychic, but a psychic was not always what they were getting. On a few occasions when a so-called psychic was ill and could not do their shift, I was asked if I had any friends who were not shy and would be happy to replace them for the night. It didn't matter if they weren't psychics; they just had to know how to make up a story in a flash and make it sound real. On top of that, they would be given some tricks of the trade on how to wing it.

I clearly remember one night a reader couldn't make it in that evening for her shift, and the producers begged us all to call our friends to see if they could organise a speedy replacement. I overheard another psychic telling her friend that it didn't matter if she wasn't a psychic, just come in anyway and make it all up. And so, she did! An hour and a half later, hair and make-up all done, the girlfriend came strolling in and, with a few nerves up her sleeve, asked me what she should do and how she should do it. She told me that she was doing her friend a favour by coming in and that she has never done anything like this before. Heck, she hadn't even seen a deck of tarot cards before either! I once again had no words. I made it clear that night how I felt about their lack of ethics, and I never returned to the studio ever again. The girlfriend did, though, each and every Saturday night after that. Her presence on line was magnetic, she basically spoke through her backside, and she winged it until she became one of the most popular psychics on the program. About 6 months down the track, she left her high-paying corporate job to become a full-time psychic. Her hypnotic charm and gift of talking rubbish meant that what she got paid in a week in the corporate world was what she was able to earn out of unsuspecting paying clients in one whole day! Not a bad day's work, huh?

One of my biggest worries about these phone lines is that you will usually find them most active after midnight when the desperate and lonely people are out. Some have addictions, whether it be to gambling, alcohol or something else, but there is no care of duty from the phone lines in order to not feed their addiction any further. These people could be using their last dollars on their credit cards to speak to a fake psychic and potentially lose all that they have left. I remember one night, one of the "healers" on the programme told someone that she would send him some of her magic vibes and heal him in an instant. The next morning, I woke up to find out that he had committed suicide that very night as soon as he got off the phone with her. There is no duty of care, and I just could not be a part of it.

Having worked in the industry for over 30 years, I saw it all, and sadly I had seen more bad than I had seen good. It seems everywhere you go, no matter what country in the world or what suburb you live in, there seems to be a psychic reading available on every street corner.

I had a customer who soon became a friend. She married well and with that never had to work a day in her life. She flaunted her wealth not in a show-off type of way, but in a way that you just knew she came from money and lots of it. One Friday morning, she came into Embrace distraught and a little overdramatic, well so I thought until I realised that this was a case for Colin, and so I had him on the phone within minutes of talking to her. The previous night she had attended a meditation night, and the organiser was a well-known Reiki master. While deep into her meditation session, the Reiki master stopped the class to let them all know that our beautiful, wonderful customer had a bad and evil spirit with her. It was bad enough that this was even mentioned to the group, but what was to take place should be criminal if only there were rules and regulations around this kind of stuff. Without even a blink of the eye, the teacher had our customer pinned to the floor, and started to perform an exorcism on this poor unsuspecting woman. I mean, she walked into the class fine and walked out a total mess. During the so-called exorcism, the Reiki master started receiving messages from the 'divine' that the bad spirit needed to leave our customer's body in order for the safety of the rest of the group. Well, they definitely forgot the safety of the customer as she had then been mob attacked, pinned to the floor and the curse of a thousand demons were forced to leave her body. However, if she was to pay a handsome amount of money for the safety of the group, the 'mob' would leave her alone.

Whilst she was relaying the experience back to me, I knew Colin needed to get involved as the energy we were dealing with was much more intense than I could have worked with. Colin took one look at her and told her that there was nothing whatsoever attached to her other than her Cartier bracelet and matching earrings and that she needed to stop the nonsense of believing so. Because the experience had shaken her to the core, she truly believed the Reiki master and therefore brought her own demons along for the ride. It took psychiatric professionals to help her in the end, but I tell this story to awaken you so that you realise that not everyone in the spiritual world has your best interests at heart. It was our customer's wallet they were interested in, and with that, they took her mind.

We know that our minds can play some powerful tricks on us, and I hope all these years later that our customer knows how wonderful and beautiful she really is. The only evil demon in the room that night was the Reiki master and the cowardly flock that brought her to her knees. I then introduced her to Janine, who invited our customer to Friday night circles. This beautiful lady now runs the circles, and after I attended the first one, I knew that our customer was now in the right hands.

You can trust me when I say that I have worked with some of the craziest people in the world. Sometimes I think I must be crazy too, but from my observations and experiences, I have come to know that there is a very fine line between being psychic and being psycho. It has always been a private joke between Colin and I. I can't help but wonder if the two sometimes go hand in hand.

I know the word "narcissist" is a trending word in the world at the moment, but I use this word because I can find no better word than this to fit the descriptions of many of the folks I have worked with who claim to be psychic. As I have said before, the louder they yell, the more they have to hide, and I already have a strong hunch on who will yell the loudest once my story is told.

226

Like insolent, spoilt bratty children who don't get their own way, they act nothing like the spiritual holier-than-thou people they portray themselves to be. From voodoo dolls to black magic, nasty untrue gossip, backstabbing, severe bullying, stealing each other's material and clients, relentless competition where it becomes a dog eat dog world, egos the size of houses, and lies upon lies. Perception is an amazing thing; however, you never really know what is real and what is not.

I have come to believe that some psychics I have met and known over the years have had some kind of mental health issues with many childhood traumas that could send anyone to their knees. I have heard story after story and began to notice the same pattern. Tate was another psychic who came to read for us for a short while. Her childhood consisted of sexual assault from a trusting neighbour, and every romantic relationship she entered into was doomed before it had even begun. A pretty young girl who knew how to cry wolf more than the boy who actually cried it. I must admit, I had a soft spot for Tate. She was a struggling single mother with a one-year-old, and I believed all the victim stories she fed me. Heck, I even babysat her children while she worked for me. Tate knew she had it good with me. We worked around her schedule, and we made her life very easy in order to earn the enormous paycheck she received from me each week. I was happy to help, as I, too, once remembered how hard it once was to be a single mother with little income.

The only problem we had with Tate is that she became a princess, and it became her way or the highway. A few times, I had to gently remind her whose business it actually was, and with that, she made her own rules, and that is when the child in her shone through a lot stronger than the woman she actually was. Tantrums were thrown, diva moments that belonged in Hollywood were displayed, and her loyal clients were let down. Time and time again, week after week, until it became month after month. I sat Tate down and told her we couldn't run a business like this, and as much as we all loved her (which we actually did), her performances were unprofessional and not only unspiritual-like but unladylike also. Tate being the typical narcissist, didn't like being told how to run 'my' show, and it became clear when her clients were getting fed up and blaming myself and my staff for Tate's unprofessionalism. Don't get me wrong; she was a good reader. She just had so many personal problems she brought to work with her when they needed to be left at the front door like everyone else's.

On one Friday afternoon, a client had booked a 3 o'clock appointment with Tate, and she drove an hour and a half away from the other side of Sydney to be there on time. Tate just happened to be having one of her diva moments and told the client after her long hot drive in the crazy Sydney traffic that she had a headache and was going home. I was mortified. I mean, we all get headaches. In fact, I have a headache right now as I type these words, but I have a commitment to you, my dear reader, and I sure am going to finish my book by the due date. The same should have gone for Tate, who had no respect for the long drive her client had taken to come to see her for a reading. Tate, in her high heels and bright red lipstick, strutted out of Embrace and left the rest of us to pick up the pieces. My mouth was left open with no words to say to this poor woman. Not only had the client driven a long, long way to get to Embrace, she also had taken the day off work to make it happen. We were the ones who bore the brunt of this unhappy woman. The wonderful professional reputation I grew for so many years was falling around my feet at the narcissist princess attitude of a psychic with absolutely no morals and very little integrity.

Stupidly, I gave Tate a second chance. Like I said, I had a soft spot for her and a need to mother her, which included fresh home-cooked meals directly from my very own kitchen. The following week was my final straw when a client showed up for her 9 am reading, and there was no sign of Tate. After 20 minutes of repeatedly calling her number, she finally answered to let me know she wasn't coming into work that day, as she had to wait for the handyman to come to install her air conditioner. With that, I told her not to come back to work ever again, and I slammed the phone down. From memory, we had to refund a whole day of clients, which was something in the vicinity of around $950, and they were the ones who didn't want to swap for another reader!

Obviously, I got blocked and deleted once again, and the gossip started around the psychic world on what a bad boss I was and how hard Tate was done by. I am not sure about you, but if you have a boss that brings you meals, babysits your children, and works rosters around to suit your lifestyle, I know for sure I would never bite the hand that fed me, whether I was on struggling street or not.

I heard from a girlfriend only last week that she had made a booking privately with Tate well over 3 months ago and was made to pay for it prior. Tate was not at home when Holly showed up for her reading, and my friend has not received her reading nor her money back to this day. It is a shame, really, as Tate truly was a good reader, but like the rest of the narcissist psychics I know, it always had to be on their terms, or it wasn't going to be at all.

Tammy also worked for us on every other Thursday and Sunday. She was a wild one with a sense of adventure and a spirit of fun. I liked her a lot, and we became friends outside of Embrace and our working world. Before long, Tammy would end up in my home hysterically in tears after yet another alcohol-infused domestic violence situation. Her partner was not the kind of man you would want to meet in a dark ally, and my home became hers. My husband, Ross, was good to her. He drove her places she needed to go when public transport was not available. He listened to her for hours upon hours as she relayed the abuse she was receiving one day after the next from a man who quite obviously had no love or respect for her or himself. Tammy struggled financially, and I recall one time when she had been evicted from her home for not paying the rent. Ross, who has always been my knight in shining armour, came to rescue as her knight in armour that day and bailed her out of the mess she had found herself in. $450 was a lot of money for us to pay her rent, but that's what you do for friends, right? Meanwhile, her husband had just blown his last paycheck at the poker machines, and while he drank down the last drops of his gin, he reminded Tammy of what a useless piece of arse she was. Both Ross and I had words with him, but it is very hard to make sense to a man who is so infused with his own demons, along with a bottle or two of gin, mixed in with a whole lot of hate for the world.

Ross and I invited Tammy to stay with us for a while until she found her feet again. I made sure extra shifts at work were given to her, and I also snuck in an extra $25 a week to pay for her cigarettes. Sadly, a few weeks later, like a lot of domestic violence women do, Tammy went back to the abuse. She was forced to stop work with me as I was now a threat to her relationship and was seen as trying to break these two love birds up. (I do say 'love birds' sarcastically here). She resigned from Embrace that very same week via text message, and once again, I was blocked and deleted. I did bump into her not that long ago, and as much as she tried to avoid me, I made sure that she couldn't. She is still living in the same domestic violent environment, she is scrambling for money each week, and she is still doing readings for clients specialising in love and money. I don't know about you, as you may think differently than me, but don't you see something so wrong here?

It is common practice these days to find a psychic on nearly every street corner you turn. If I am at an event, sure enough, a psychic will be there. If I am in a restaurant, there will be one there too. I turn on the television, and lo and behold, another psychic with their fake predictions and even faker personalities that match the fake certificates they carry around with them. Call me harsh or judgmental, but too many years of dealing with this sort of behaviour tends to make one a little harder.

I feel sad when I tell you that even psychics have two faces the same way a coin does. From where I stand, I cannot help but feel sceptical when I see psychics not only speaking to your dead relatives or predicting the future, which can be changed the moment you step outside of their reading, but also now cashing in on the woo-hoo wellness industry. Many have now rebranded themselves as "intuitive" or "intuitive healers" who channel "energy" to help people in order for them to have better lives and promote kindness projects.

Just do yourself one favour next time one of these intuitive healers or psychics crosses your path… make sure they have their house in order before they try to clean yours!

Chapter 11

When Earth Angels Meet Hell's Angels

"Those that yell the loudest have the most to hide."

Let me start this chapter by telling you that I do believe in Earth Angels. I, for one, have been lucky enough to know them through beautiful souls as Colin, Helen and Janine. Born in human form, they are not only humble, but they share with generosity their love, light, and kindness in a world that is sometimes a bit hard to live in.

I truly believe that each and every one of us shares the light of God inside of us, but I know through my very own experiences these Earth Angels shine their light a lot brighter, and their vibration is much higher. They have been sent by God to share, help, heal and save our planet from pretty much ourselves.

On the other hand, there is also a bit of hell's angels in all of us too. That part of our soul, if we let it, can turn dark and take us to a place where we really don't want to be. Our ego takes over, our anger and resentment over life's unfairness still churn deep within us, and we long to be something better than what we are and anything other than what we are. Our deepest wounds become the catalyst of the need to prove ourselves better, even though we don't know how. We can't get our own shit together, so we decide to get other people's lives in order instead.

The perfect way to deceive somebody is first to deceive yourself, and therefore finding a career in the psychic world fits the prescription of stroking the ego of a fragile personality who desperately needs validation. A lot of psychics, healers, so-called shamans, Reiki masters, mediums blah blah blah fit the bill perfectly and sadly, I have met them all. In no way am I suggesting that all psychics, mediums, healers, shamans are not the real deal. I am not even trying to imply that either. I am just saying that throughout my career, I have met both the good, bad, ugly, pretty and anything in between.

I am sure you have all seen the gifted clairvoyant who has been practicing for over 20 years and is always a fourth-generation psychic whose great grandmother possessed the "gift." The gift of BS, that is what I call it. Or the psychic who suddenly woke up one morning being able to read all the minds in her workplace whilst predicting the next big crash of the stock market. I guess we can throw the very talented medium in there who started to hear voices one day and, instead of being medicated, started to make loads of dollars instead. I, for one, am very sceptical when claims are made by these people. Even though a lot of psychics absolutely come from a long line of psychics in their family, there are also just as many who claim they do but actually don't.

No wonder it is hard for the true lightworkers to be taken seriously. I have said it before, and I will say it again that there is most definitely, without a doubt, a very fine line between psychic and psycho. The perfect palette for a fake psychic consists of many things, but the first and foremost is always their own belief that they have a special gift. Most of their art is a mixture of spending a lot of time on social media, lots of sizing people up, working out the body language, and adding a fragrance of incense here and a touch of theatrics there. A true scam and neither the fake psychic nor the client knew it!

Most of the time, the psychic just gives their client the fantasy and happy-ever-after that they so desperately need to hear, and that will keep the psychic booked out for the next twelve months. I also know of psychics who are also booked a year in advance, but their souls are so pure, their work so amazingly accurate and their hearts in the right places, and I need to clarify that these are not the ones I am referring to here. It is impossible for the untrained eye to see, but for an old veteran like myself, it is as plain as the writing on the wall.

It saddens me to my core to see many people hooked in like this, but I also have found our industry a great hook for paedophiles and sexual predators. You remember the story I told you earlier about my girlfriend's partner who was on parole for paedophilia and yet was healing people at a popular spiritual fair? Sadly, his is not the only story I can tell. It embarrasses me to say that Embrace has been guilty of employing what we would say in plain English "a dirty old man." He portrayed himself as a modern-day Shaman (don't even get me started on that one), with a healing touch and a psychic ability that suddenly came to him one day through a miraculous intervention between his spirit guide, his soul, and the small amount of weed he was smoking.

He was a master in disguise and, as Ross would call him, a jack of all trades but a master of none. He had an enormous ego that coincided well with his acting skills and gibberish nonsense that came out of his mouth. He had us all fooled for some time but deep inside me from the first day he was employed, I knew something just wasn't right. The problem was, I couldn't pin it down to anything, and it took not only a disaster that was waiting to happen to work it all out but also Colin with a cheesy grin saying, "I told you so!"

At first, everyone thought the new kid (sorry, shaman) on the block was the ant's pants. Everyone, that is, except for Colin. At first glance, Colin looked at him, then at me, and in his famous words, cried out, "Hooley Dooley." Followed by a "put your guard up and don't let the dark outshine the light." Before walking out of the store, shaking his head in laughter, Colin looked back and said, "Don't say I didn't warn you about this one."

The psychic shaman was charming, alluring, enticing, and captivating. He knew his stuff, but it was really the theatrics that sold him. After some time, I started to get some complaints about him. One woman by the name of Suzy emailed me a long-enthralled letter on how she felt she was being groomed by the shaman, and how he made her feel like she was only good for one thing, and that was to have sex with him in the name of spirituality. Please let me be the first to tell you that if ever, and I mean ever, this has happened to you, or God forbid it ever does, please go to the authorities first and foremost. In other words, this Shaman believed that his penis was so powerful that it could heal her! He most definitely had a magic wand, and boy was it doing lots of work!

Another woman rang me in tears, saying that he insisted she come to his house after work in order for him to offer her proper healing without any interruptions in a space that would be safe and quiet. I tell you now, she ran out as fast as she could when her intuition kicked in, and she realised that he only had her there for one thing. The moment he told her that her base chakra was blocked and he needed to unblock it, that was her cue to run. The saddest part about this is that his wife knew exactly what he was doing, but she didn't mind, as his income was giving her a lifestyle that most other women would dream of.

I finally had to have a difficult and awkward conversation with him to let him know that his magic wand wasn't really that magical, that he was no longer fooling me, and that I cannot and will not accept this behaviour in my beautiful shop. Once he knew that I knew about his magical penis and what he was up to, he resigned the next day via text message. He blocked and deleted me on all social channels and started a story that I was an unethical person to work for, and that is why he had no choice other than to leave Embrace. It's OK, I knew the truth, and that is all that mattered. Needless to say, Colin and Ross had to come in for damage control as I felt so badly responsible to all the clients and for falling for the shaman's nonsense in the first place.

Let me get one thing clear as I repeat myself over and over again... Being psychic in no way means that you are spiritual! To be a spiritual being, you must first and foremost have the recognition and belief that there is something much greater than yourself. An all-powered higher Being, and that the world and life we live in is a part of cosmic and divine nature. A spiritual person is someone whose highest priority in this lifetime is to love others and care for people, animals, and our Mother Earth. They understand that we are all One and make every attempt in their lives to honour this oneness with unity and wholeness.

I find that a lot of people get being religious and being spiritual confused and think that they are one and the same. This is not true. I know plenty of religious people who go to Church on Sunday, say their prayers, and still manage to involve themselves in malicious gossip with nasty personalities throughout their week. They are outright mean and righteous and don't practice what they preach. Just look at the scandal in the Catholic Church, and I rest my case. Of course, though, somebody can be both religious and spiritual, and I know plenty. They believe in their religion, but they are open to the religion of others and the acceptance that we are all different yet still the same.

I have some very close Muslim friends who are so devoted to their faith, but their lives are spiritual, not religious because they live their lives from their hearts and souls and are not tied up in the dogma of their religion. They have accepted my family and me into their lives, and we have accepted them into ours, and together we all have a wonderful friendship based on respect.

I also know loads of yoga, meditation teachers, and people who belong to a spiritual group or spiritual church who are in no way no how spiritual by any sense of the word. I have been in circles where they bitch about the other, about the way she dresses or styles her hair, how she mothers her children or how many times she lacks saying the word Namaste. They have no loving thoughts or actions in their normal lives, or they devotedly follow the teachings of what they practice but still are judgmental of others. They are jealous of others more successful than themselves, and they compete on who is more spiritual or psychic or more popular than they. They even compare notes on who has more clients at their classes and workshops.

I also know of many people who do not go to church, they don't follow a religion, pray, meditate or belong to a spiritual group, yet they are some of the most spiritual people I know. Without a second thought, they are the ones who will do anything for another person. They want to help, they do help, and they do with love and a whole lot of Zen in their hearts. They are kind to others, and they do not judge others. They have a softness in their eyes, and you know that in their presence they embody the wholeness of what we are here on this planet for, even if they don't know it themselves.

I know psychics who have started kindness, and gratitude projects and life-changing workshops but who, in no form of the word, are anywhere near kind, grateful, or have their lives together in any form or shape. Patrina was one such reader who only worked at Embrace for a short while until I had to ask her to leave. She would come out of her readings laughing at how stupid her clients were, and telling the staff and anyone else who wanted to listen all about her clients' personal lives. She was racist towards Muslims and would have many horrible things to say about their religion without doing any homework of her own to actually educate herself. Patrina liked to call all the other readers in the store "street corner readers" because she had a university degree, and they didn't. I'm not sure about you, but the universities we have here in Sydney definitely don't offer psychic classes, and you most definitely don't need any university degree to be one. Needless to say, Patrina, in all her ego, opened a kindness program in order to help make the world a better place and to help people change their lives for the better. As long as you weren't Muslim, you were allowed to join. I didn't even hesitate when I fired Patrina. Not one form of racism of any kind was allowed in my store, in my presence, or in my space and I wanted no part of it.

Occasionally I see articles in the newspapers about Patrina and her kindness project, and I just shake my head and sigh.

I have always believed that only love exists and can never die. God is love, and so am I, so are you. Anything other than love, like fear, anxiety, unhappiness, lies, meanness, is not a part of our God force. When we pray, whether it be to God, Allah, our guardian angels, the goddess in all her magnificence, the elements of the Earth, or to many different gods, the essence is all about allowing the spirit of love, peace, joy, truth, and kindness into your hearts and to guide you in all your thoughts and actions throughout your life.

Just because someone is a yoga or meditation teacher, a tarot card reader or psychic, a medium or someone who teaches these things does not mean in any way that they have invited love into their hearts and the God force into their lives. Trust me when I say that I have seen it all, I have met them all, I have worked with them and even socialized with them. I have learnt from them, and I have taught them, and by no means does it equate that what they are doing is for the highest good of all and our planet.

Let me tell you a story... Once upon a time, about three years ago to be exact, I had a nightmare, and when I awoke, I found myself pinned down to my bed, and I could not move or speak. A black cloud covered me, and whilst Ross snored his head off, I was trapped in some gooey, grey matter that was making my head spin and my stomach churn. I called on the white light, but it wouldn't come. I tried to say the Lord's Prayer, but it wouldn't pass my lips. I tried to wake my husband, but he wouldn't stir. I knew at that moment I was under a psychic attack. I mustered all my strength to sit up, yell at the top of my lungs, "Fuuuuck Off," and called on my spirit guides for help. At that, Ross awoke, and after I told him what I had just experienced, he put his arms around me, told me it was all a bad dream, and stroked my hair until I fell asleep.

The very next morning, I came to work to open my doors of Embrace at 9 am to find a big black dead bird at my doorstep. I knew the moment I saw it that it was no coincidence that it just happened to die on my doorstep. I also knew by the energy around it that some serious hexing and cursing was being done on Embrace by another powerful and well-established business that was viewing Embrace as a direct threat to theirs. I mean, Embrace is in the heart of a huge shopping centre, and there was no possible way that the big black crow flew into the centre and chose to land at our doorstep when it had 300 other shops to choose from.

It was time to call in the big guns once again. The energy around this was so dark and heavy that I didn't feel strong enough that day to deal with it on my own. Besides, I was very much rattled by the whole incident, and the look on that dead bird's face made me feel like I was the lead in my very own horror movie. Colin and Janine to the rescue, and with the power of three, we did some pretty heavy magic that day. Of course, my inquisitive mind wanted to know who did this and why. Colin told me not to worry about the whys, whilst Janine told me to let it go and bind it whilst sending it back with love and light. Stuff that! My dark side wanted to play that day, and there was no way that love and light were being sent back to where it had come from. "This is war," I yelled as every part of my body was shivering with nerves and hysteria. I wanted revenge, and Colin just had to look at me once to put me back into a state of accepting and letting go.

I eventually found out who placed the dead crow at Embrace's doorstep, and that person is a woman I have never met. She decided that her clothing business was not doing well so she would copy Embrace and change her business to be like ours. Even though it was situated in amongst a complex of shops in a small suburb about 20 minutes away, neither of us was any threat to each other. Well, that is what I thought anyway. Penny decided to also teach love and light and all that BS. She also made a mistake during a psychic development class to insult Embrace to the students attending. For some reason, she then went on to tell her students that I was not a nice person and whatever else that rocked her boat. Student after student reported back to me and my staff what was being said, and for once, I told everyone at Embrace to just ignore it. Penny had even started to poach my psychics; some went to work with her, some did not. Those that did come back to Embrace and realised the grass is not greener on the other side of the Shire.

Penny also made the mistake of sending me an email in which she threatened to take legal action against me if I continued to run events that she believed belonged to her even though I had been running them nine years prior. Apparently, I had copied her, so I deserved to be hexed! Go figure!

You have no idea how much I wanted to send all that energy back to this woman and her shop on the morning the dead bird greeted me on my doorstep. The dark side of me wanted retribution, and for the rest of that day, I planned out in my head the best plan of attack. I was furious, hurt, confused and outraged. Admittedly, I didn't like this side of me, but the sheer audacity of someone claiming to be so mightier than thou, doing this was really rattling me to my core. After calming down later that day, doing a massive binding ritual with Janine and Colin, and putting myself back into my body, I understood the meaning of it all. Even though it was an outright attack on me and everything I had worked so hard to achieve, I finally understood that the battle between light and dark will always be a constant in my life for as long as I chose to do this work. I realised I would be tested over and over again until I learnt the art of no reaction.

As for Penny, she is still there, still talking about me and my business and still finding it necessary to feel threatened by everything we do. She is also still teaching psychic development classes and life coaching and teaching people about how to be better people. And just like in any other business, for yours to succeed, I took my father's advice and just concentrated on my own. The fact that Penny was more engaged in Embrace than in hers was what became her detriment.

I also had the non-pleasure of working with a very powerful psychic who would use fear tactics with her clients to get them coming back week after week. She earned big bucks and bragged about how very lucrative her cash stash under the mattress was becoming. She had this way of convincing people that she had first-hand connections with the Divine, and she was chosen well and above everyone else to deliver the messages of doom and gloom. Firstly, Spirit will never give us messages of death and disaster as light only knows light, and its energy does not flow in any other direction. The Divine, or God or whatever you want to call it, does not work in this manner, and yet Dania had them all fooled. In order for no more bad luck to enter their lives, and with the handover of a few hundred dollars in a matter of 30 minutes, she could make it all go away.

I sat with Dania on a lunch break once at a spiritual fair and asked her how she was able to generate so many clients even though her reputation was still fairly new. She explained in full detail that if she has them coming back in fear, she is promised a lifetime of financial security whilst still collecting welfare payments and child support. As she packed up the remains of her lunch to take with her back to her workspace, she finished stating, "It works. You should try it." With that, my mouth fell open, and I was turned off the rest of my lunch.

It was only a year ago that I received a random text message from Dania. I hadn't seen her in years, and she felt the need to pass on a message that the Divine had given her about me.

Three months later, I was watching a movie with my friends, something I rarely get a chance to do, and I received a random text message from Dania. I had never thought of her since that spiritual fair and thought it bizarre that she should be messaging me late on a Saturday night. A well-known fact within the clique is that Dania is not one to shy away from smoking a joint or two every day, and she was not ashamed to admit it. I opened my message to be warned that she had just been given a message from the Divine that I was in some serious trouble. My business was about to go broke, Ross was going to leave me, and all my friends would turn on me, and I would end up in a nut home.

Moving forward years later and it was quite evident that the Divine who was speaking to Dania during her stoned induced state was definitely not the same Divine that I speak

251

to. Always be warned when a psychic tells you they have a message from up above because if it is a negative one, then you know firsthand they are not getting their information from the light. Full stop.

What I am about to say is as true as the sky is blue, and even now, sometimes I find I need to pinch myself to make sure even I am not making it up. Many years ago, it was a Thursday night at Embrace, and I just had the weirdest feeling something was not right. The sensation stayed with me for a long time, so I called Colin and asked him what was going on. He was at my store not long after and told me that we needed to go back to my apartment. Obviously, I questioned why, and he just very casually told me that this was no time for questions. I should have known better anyway to question anything that Colin did or said.

As we opened the door to my high-rise apartment on the 7th floor, we just stood there. I was quiet and looking at Colin with that stance as if to say, "Well, what do we do next?" I didn't need to verbalise my thoughts as he read my mind, and just like that, he said, "It's OK, Maxine, you can come out now." WTF was going on, and why was Maxine in my apartment?

With that, Maxine walked out of my children's room with her head down and tears streaming down her eyes. I had no idea what she was doing there, how she got in there, and why she was there. I truly thought this was one big joke that everyone else was involved in and somehow forgot to tell me. You see, I thought the history between her and I had finished with the spiritual fair saga, but here she was again, this time in my very own lounge room. As far as she was concerned, I was not spiritual, and she was much more spiritual than I would ever be, so somehow, she felt the need to do God knows what in my home whilst I was not there.

Before I could say anything, and way before I could even think to say something, I felt Colin's energy change. I got a little scared, and as I stepped out of his energy field and into a corner where I could see what on earth was going on, I noticed Colin's eyes changing. Actually, his whole body was changing, and just like that, I realised then and there that what I was seeing was real. I just froze. His eye's started to turn from brown to blue. So blue, in fact, that I could have swum in them with no return. From there, his face changed, and even though I could tell it was still Colin, I knew I was witnessing either a divine miracle or that I had accidentally ingested a whole heap of magic mushrooms in my salad that I had brought for lunch that day.

Considering no magic mushrooms were on the menu at my local café, I had no other explanation than a divine miracle. Suddenly, something was growing out of Colin's back, and thinking it was his spirit guide, I quickly came to realise that that something was wings. Yes, I said it. Wings! I was trying hard to wake up, but I was very awake, and I don't think I will ever be more awake than I was that day. His wings wrapped around me, and I was lifted into the air like a flying blanket that was taking me on a magical ride. His wings encompassed the whole of my living room, and it was truly the first time in my life that I can say I saw my very first angel.

Meanwhile, Maxine was not acting alone. She, along with her accomplice, someone who I had held dear to my heart, both started to also transform. Angels were far from what they were turning into, and instead of the immaculate eyes of Colin's, theirs had turned a green snakey lizard-like shape. Colin's roar was loud and deafening, and with his words, "There is the door, I advise you to GET OUT," they both turned to look at me once more as they stepped out, and both their tongues in perfect unison formed the shape of a fork, and a huge "hiss" was heard. By the time I looked back at Colin, his eyes were brown once more, and he was the Colin I had always known. He knew without asking that I was in shock and was questioning what I had just witnessed. He wrapped his arms around me and told me that I am forever protected, and they would never try to harm me ever again. He was right, they never did.

For a long while, Colin and I never spoke about that night. I didn't know how to bring it up, and even though he knew that, I knew he had been waiting for me to speak of it first. When I finally was ready to talk about it, Colin's words shook me to the core, and I knew he was right, "You can spend your whole life never being awake," and I knew I had finally once and for all woken up to a lifetime of sleeping.

In this place we call Earth, a person either has integrity, or they lack integrity. Integrity is like virginity, you can't sacrifice it and then retain it. Once it is gone, it is gone. It is as simple as that. I remember my fairy godmother, Helen, once telling me that integrity is not something you show to others but rather something you do behind their back. Over the three decades working in the spiritual industry, I have seen and witnessed a lot, and very sadly, integrity is something I haven't seen a lot of. It was after Helen's words that I decided then and there that I was going to waste no more time arguing about who was a good person and who was not. I was just going to be a good person with a kind heart.

Please don't get me wrong, I do not claim it to be easy when you have been the target of bullying and betrayal. It hurts so deep into your core that you will never understand the reasons why some people can be so cruel and get away with it. When you're an empath like me, it is even harder. I have lived my life expecting people to be like me, and with that expectation always comes disappointment.

Laughter has been my medicine, and I have always had the gift of finding something to laugh about even when there really is nothing to laugh about. I guess that is why I became an avid Seinfeld fan and couldn't wait to visit the soup kitchen when I visited New York. My cousin and I even found laughter smack bang in the middle of our grandfather's funeral. It was definitely no laughing matter, but when the priest asked the congregation to stand in "fear" and there was a big, massive, hairy, huntsman spider above our heads, we did more than fear. We laughed whilst our parents scolded us, and that big spider ran off to breed more big hairy spiders.

When "Star Wars" first came out in nineteen seventy-something, I remember my father taking us as a family to watch it, and the movie became an enigma in my childhood home. I was hooked on the saga between light and dark, and even though I was nine years old, I was wise enough to understand the symbolism in it and the comparisons to life itself. For eons, our world has always had the fight between dark and light, good and bad, evil and virtue. We have our Earth angels, and we have Hell's angels, and all you need to do is choose what side you want to be on.

When Yoda, the small green humanoid alien in Star Wars, who is powerful with the Force and served as Grandmaster of the Jedi order spoke the words, "Fear is the path to the dark side. Fear leads to anger. Anger leads to hate. Hate leads to suffering," I understood his message. His words rang through deep after reading a letter I received in the mail, and I finally understood once and for all the battle between the Earth angels and the Hell's angels.

257

It wasn't the words in the letter that upset me, it was the meanness, nastiness, and hatred that someone had in their heart for another human being. Somebody wanted my beautiful store Embrace closed, and they were going to stop at nothing to make it happen. I couldn't understand, with all the good we were offering to our community and the hearts we were touching in such a positive way, that someone wanted to destroy all that good. We always offered a lot of free services to people in need, products to enhance the lives and families of our customers, tools to give them some hope and strength when life got too tough, magic in the lives of the children who entered our doors, and most importantly big massive mamma bear hugs which we have become very known for. It truly is a beautiful space, even if I may say so myself!

Let me finish this chapter by sharing with you a copy of that letter:

"Dear Rosie,

What a wonderful woman you are. You may think that you are so great with a successful business and FESTIVAL OF DREAMS, but I am here to remind you of the opposite. You are a completely dumbass woman with dark evil eyes, and you look like a dark witch. You also look tired, stressed.

I have a lot of connections in our area, and I will be telling all my contacts I know not to go to your shop, and I will send them to your rival.

You do not have a great reputation, and you are not a spiritual person nor should you be running a spiritual business. You have attitude and not many people like you. Nobody likes you or thinks the sun shines out of you the way you do. Despite how you talk yourself up you are not a successful businesswoman at all. You are uneducated and unintelligent, that's plain to see.

You are just a fat little leb girl that whinges, manipulates and cries just to get your own way. So many people are aware of these ugly traits of yours and you are talked about as a complete joke.

Speaking of ugly, my goodness all the money you have spent and wasted on botox and collagen. How much do you spend on looking as bad as you do with fake lips, botox, fake hair and eyebrows. It's certainly no enhancement to your big ears, big nose, big earrings and big hips. What a disaster of a woman you are. I despise people like you. You look ridiculous, you stupid little person. Your ridiculous earrings are nearly as big as your egotistical fat head. Let's face it, you are a fat short ass bitch that doesn't care about anyone except yourself. You are a dark two-faced woman. You really are ugly on the outside and inside – horrible person.

When it's all over, you can crawl back into your hole where you came from, and we won't have to see your boring and ridiculous face anymore. You can't even be a decent mother – such a failure on so many levels.

Go play with crystals all day, little fat girl because all the beauty work isn't working for you, and let successful people move ahead in this world.

I am looking forward to the day when your shop shuts down permanently. "

I know who wrote the letter, and with that, I closed it up, said a prayer for her, and promised myself to always stand in the truth and light. No one was going to bully, betray, harass or turn on me ever again. My fairy godmother Helen told me to burn the letter and let it go, Colin told me to use it as toilet paper, and Janine told me to bind it, but instead, I framed it

260

and hung it on my office wall as it empowered me each and every day to become a much better person. Karma always knows everybody's address, and the writer was the one who had to close her business down in the end.

And so, I find it only fitting to quote the famous words of Yoda himself, "When you look at the dark side, careful you must be. For the dark side looks back."

Chapter 12

Boss Lady

"I never lose. I either win or learn."

There are many reasons why I decided very early in my life to work for myself. I was always ambitious and loved nothing more than to compete against myself each time a new challenge came my way. I wanted a good life, a life with the flexibility that working for yourself can create. I created my own career opportunities at a time when the market was still new in both Christmas decorations and crystals, and I took a massive leap of faith and jumped right in at the grass root levels. I saw a niche, and I went for it knowing that the biggest regret I would have in my life was the risk I didn't take. With all of my heart and soul, I also wanted to help people and make a difference in this world. I never doubted my destiny from the moment the hand of Jesus touched my soul and gave me a glimpse into my future when I was just a child. I had this crazy idea that I would be so rich that I could save the world from all its poverty and homelessness.

I knew I had a solution to people's problems and also knew that it would be a sin in my world if I did not go with my God-given gifts.

However, it isn't always easy being self-employed, but I must admit that the psychological benefits outweighed any downfalls I had about being my own boss. Over the years, I enjoyed the freedom, flexibility, and control of making my own money, working at my own schedule instead of somebody else's, and giving myself and my staff job roles that not only aligned with our strengths and weaknesses but also coincided with something we loved to do.

I promised myself I would be a good and fair boss, and I always kept that promise. I remember clearly the first day of my very first job outside of the family business. It was a summer day in 1986, and I was very nervous. With my padded shoulders and high heels, I walked into the prestige offices of the 16th floor in the AMP building, overlooking the magnificent view of Sydney Harbour. I was anxious, nervous, excited and bewildered all rolled into one. It took one introduction to my boss, Bev B, and all of a sudden, a wave of immediate calm swept over me, and I knew I was in

263

the right place. She was kind, and her eyes showed it, and she was maternal yet strong. She took me in under her wing, and even when I made mistakes, she never yelled, made me feel bad, or embarrassed me in front of other colleagues. She was my boss, and yet sometimes she would shout me out for champagne and smoked salmon lunch or bring me in my morning coffee. She sometimes even told me about her weekends that consisted of a lifestyle I had only dreamed about at 17. Her eyes still pierce through my psyche when I think of her, and to date, no google search has been able to help me find her. Bev B left a big impact on me, and I promised myself that when it was time for me to be a boss, I would be every bit as kind and wonderful as Bev B. I kept my promise, and that was good, but sadly not everybody was an employee like me. Because Bev B was such a fair and great boss, I actually wanted to bend over backwards and do anything she asked of me.

I learnt very quickly that if you want to climb the ladder in the corporate world, you do whatever it takes to succeed. If your boss gave you a manuscript to type at 5 pm on a Friday night, you would stay back with no questions asked and do it. If you had to work through your lunch break, you just did that too. I learnt here on the 16th floor that success is what you give, not what you take. It took me six weeks from when I first started in that position to be promoted, and another three months after that for another promotion. I worked my way to the top, sometimes taking work home with me and never once questioning about overtime or checking my clock to see if it was going home time. Those who succeeded with me in the corporate world were the same people who were also giving up their Friday nights or their hot lunch dates. I began earning a lot more money because I had been recognised as a good employee, and it was then that I also had my first taste of jealousy in the workforce.

Working in the family retail store and having my father as my boss taught me a hell of a lot too. I learnt that as soon as a customer walked into the store, you drop everything, including your apple turnover cream puffs (the ones my uncle used to make me buy), and attend to our customer. I learnt how to read the body language of potential thieves and upsell any item we had in store. I talked to people from all different walks of life. I even served Mel Gibson a pair of beach thongs before he became THE Mel Gibson. It was here in the family business I found my first crush, a young musician who lived downstairs from the family store, and even though nothing ever happened, I at least developed the courage to say "Hello."

I guess you can say that work ethics ran in my veins, and my father set me up the right foundations to work myself up the corporate ladder in what was, in the mid-'80s, a very male-dominated world. I just expected that everybody would hold this standard of high ethics in their workplace, but it became quite evidently clear that when I became the boss, my expectations left me to be disappointed.

In Embrace's early days when we did the weekly payroll, I had an enormous amount of satisfaction knowing that I was responsible for the success of my staff, for food on their table, and for providing them with a working environment that worked around their lifestyles, all within the name of the Embrace family. My ideas, my aspirations, and my dreams provided each and every one of my staff an opportunity to earn a living, provide for their family and fulfil their own dreams. I never asked for anything in return other than loyalty and honesty.

Being self-employed is hard work, yet it is very satisfying, especially knowing that every single day the doors of Embrace remained open, I was helping others and doing what I absolutely loved. I also wanted to have control over my own destiny and to make money. Lots of it!

There I said it, the "M" word. God forbid someone spiritual like me actually enjoys making money and spending lots of money. A common belief in the spiritual field is that money and spirituality do not mix. They believe that money is bad, and I am here to tell you that this is far from the truth. When used consciously, money can be a powerful spiritual tool and can be used for so much good, just as equal to how much evil it can be used for also.

Money can be used for so many wonderful things like purchasing food vans that go around feeding the homeless or the charity kitchens I have worked with, who cook for the parents of sick children so they won't have to eat that horrible hospital food.

With all of that being said, I saw no wrong in making money through Embrace. Our products and services only just added beauty into people's lives. We offered them hope and touched their lives in ways you cannot imagine. We provided products that would enhance their already unhappy lives; we provided an honest, safe service where clients knew they would be protected and not judged, and we held a space for people to be who they really are. To me, this is not a bad thing at all, but yet, none of this could have been nowhere near possible if it wasn't for the almighty dollar. I needed money to set it all up, I needed cash flow to pay the staff wages, and, of course, we needed funds to buy stock to fill the store.

Whether you like it or not, we live in a consumerist society, and so you have no other choice than to accept that money is a part of our story here in our Western world. We live in houses in the city, not huts in the wilderness. We need to feed our kids and buy groceries, and money gives us the opportunity to do so. We have air conditioning for our hot Aussie summers that kill us with its heat and warmth for those cold wintery nights with running hot water and the comforts of Netflix and Uber Eats. I have had the luxury of travelling the world, seeing countries that I learnt about in textbooks, cultures that were so different from mine, and the diversity that came with them.

I, for one, am grateful for all these things money has been able to provide for me. Each time a sale comes through my cash register at Embrace or through our online orders, I never forget to say a silent "Thank you."

I like the good things in life. I was brought up in a family that had spoilt me, so I guess you could say I had a bit of a silver spoon in my mouth. By the time I moved into the big wide world and learnt to fend for myself, I began to experience the reality that if you want to survive in this world, you need money to do it. I moved out of my parents' home and finally experienced what it was like to live on the poverty line. All of a sudden, there was rent and bills to pay and life to live, and because I had a contrast to the life with the safety and security of my parents, I knew which side of the fence I wanted to play in. Until the time in our evolution when money will no longer be applicable, and we as humans will be living more harmonious community living and be more in touch with our planet, as loving and caring human beings, till then I will vote to have money in my pocket each and every time.

People who believe that money is bad will always have a hard time creating financial abundance in this life, and

I believe that is why a lot of psychics I know tend to fit into this category. These people believe that to be on a spiritual path, money is not good, yet they fail to understand that their judgements of people with money are their own inner projections and fears. Instead of having a consciousness of togetherness, they have a separation consciousness, and this is what causes the problems in today's world around money, not money itself. They cannot be happy for others more successful than themselves, and they do not understand the laws of destiny, yet they preach and workshop it like it is the hidden grail.

I have found it easier to attract money because I have learnt to love money. Along with gratitude and appreciation, I have always kept my heart open to having it in my life. Money is energy, and because spirituality is about expansion, it makes sense that money is too. I do not wish to elaborate much more in this chapter on the spiritual side of having money, as I will leave that for my next book, but my aim is to give you an insight into the amazing and wonderful things I have been able to do because I have had the money to do it with. I have never believed that poverty is a virtue because in the world I live in, it is not!

I'm really not a cliché kind of a person, but I gotta tell you that when they say there are no friends in business, they really do mean that there are no friends in business! During the early years of Santa's Little Painters, I was still naïve in the business world and found myself becoming swindled by my accountant and a woman who I thought was my friend. I learnt from many mistakes along the way, and I learnt that when you are in business for yourself, there is no room to repeat the same mistakes twice. That is what I call entrepreneurial suicide.

My first mistake was trusting a woman who lived in the apartment above mine and who was also a very close friend. We spent many nights over bottles of champagne pouring our hearts and souls out to each other as each glass poured more and more dreams for our future and our lives. Nanette knew everything about me and I about her, other than she was not to be trusted. I loved her dearly, and we spoke of ourselves in old age, still drinking wine on a Friday night and reminiscing all the wonderful things life had to offer us. Nanette knew me so well to the extent that she also knew how much money I was making in my Christmas business. It didn't take long for her to want some of what I was having. The only problem was that Nanette didn't want to work for it.

She came to work for me during the 6-week Christmas period, and I paid her in cash over the silly season. And silly it was. Not understanding the full implications of paying cash in hand, I found myself many months later in the courtroom being accused of not paying her at all. I also had to answer to the Australian Taxation Office, which was absolutely no fun and something I would never want to do again. This experience cost me a lot of money, and it cost me my pride, but it also gained me a lot of wisdom to never make the same mistake again.

Fast forward to 2010, when I opened Embrace, I was swamped with psychic after psychic, only wanting to work for cash-in-hand payments. It was impossible. I wasn't going to ruin the years I had worked to get to the opening of Embrace's doors by making the same mistake twice. Plus, by this stage, a little more grown-up and a hell of a lot wiser, I knew it was illegal to pay cash in hand especially knowing that a lot of these psychics were also collecting government welfare payments. Hence began the journey of being a boss and learning that there truly are no friends in business. Well, let me actually rephrase that, there can be friends in business, but that is when those friends do not want what you are having!

I also learnt that for as long as I was a boss, I was always going to be painted with the same brush of being unfair, unethical, mean, greedy, unprofessional, and whatever else I was called that I didn't know about behind my back.

Let me just have a moment here with you as I still try to understand the reasoning. I was someone who refused to pay cash in hand to my readers who were collecting money from the government, all the while portraying themselves to be spiritual, and they became the victim! Was I missing something here? Me, the boss, became known as the unethical one by doing the legally right thing. Go figure! In psychic circles far and wide, I earned the reputation of being unspiritual and money-hungry only.

I understood to work in a place like Embrace, that it would generate the kind of staff who already had an interest in crystals and spirituality. I just didn't realise that their idea of spirituality was one-sided, especially when I had to make some tough calls for my business. I also didn't comprehend how they could believe that the Universe just provided, without the hard work it needed for the provisions to come. I blame a lot of the law of attraction gurus for this because let me tell you, it doesn't come that easy.

Paying rent in a Westfield shopping centre is also no mean feat. As a business person, you cannot just open a store, pay enormous rent, have your life and home mortgaged to the hills, and expect the business to survive without proper structures in place. Everybody in retail knows the peak seasons and the low, and we work accordingly around that. Casual staff are put off in order to compensate for the quiet times, and it is during this time that stock just cannot be brought. When money is tight, then so is the boss. Trying to explain this to staff, though, was like trying to explain to a crocodile why it was not cool to eat people! Don't get me wrong; I hated having to change rosters as it not only meant that someone's pay that week was a little less than the last, but it also meant that I was the one that would have to work on the floor instead of volunteering at my children's canteen duty.

I sacrificed a lot in Embrace's early years, including time away from my baby twins. Late nights became the norm and early mornings killed me with a passion. I had a great manager, Angelina, by my side during these first five years until she left me for a short time to have a baby. It would be a running joke amongst us girls that I would always be the last to know when one of them was pregnant as I never knew whether to congratulate them with joy or wonder why on earth would they want to!

Angelina came from a similar family business background to mine and understood the word loyalty and integrity. Over the years, as the business transformed, so did Angelina's role, and she is still very much an integral part of Embrace today as she was all those years ago.

At no point in my career did I ever expect my staff to either do something I would not do or to work the way I was. I made sure at every turn they were being paid for overtime or reimbursed with their choice of Embrace products or a shout-out for a nice meal. I provided a fridge in our back room, which I stocked with water, snacks, milk, tea, and coffee. I even brought in home-cooked meals. I ensured that all my psychics did not pay a daily rental fee for the rooms they were using, and instead, I took a commission from the actual readings they did in a day. I found this fair and much more viable for them than it was for me.

I had a vision of Embrace always being a family, and for a long while, we were, and it soon turned into my first home. The team we had was exceptional, and not only were we girls in monthly sync with each other, but we also had each other's backs and became a tight-knit bunch. That was until the day Embrace was raped. It took only one to commit the crime, but many more after that decided to join in on the gang bang.

Do you remember me telling you about Melody, the masturbating psychic? Well, she very quickly, in her role with us, started a mutiny in our beautiful store amongst the other readers on how greedy I was for taking money from their readings. Not only did they get free rent for the day in my store that I was paying extraordinary rent for, I was also spending quite a significant amount of money on the psychics for advertising, promotions, bookings, and time taken up by my staff. Embrace was responsible for the clients that came through the door, and anyone with half a business mind on their shoulders would understand that you don't steal clients behind your boss's back. But apparently, in the spiritual world, it is OK to do so, as having a conscience did not apply to these people.

I had a lot of damage control after Melody started her malicious chitchat amongst the other readers. Some left only to beg for their jobs back again many months after they found it hard to get work, and some stayed. The ones who stayed understood and appreciated what Embrace and I were doing for them. The ones who left created many stories about what a money-hungry mogul I was and how I was trying to exploit their fake gifts. My staff were too strong for Melody's poison to break through their veins and unbeknown to me, they had their own private faceoff with her when my back was turned. Simona was a customer from the very inception of Embrace. She would always come in for a chat, have some readings with our psychics and buy a few crystals and some incense here and there. She seemed nice enough, and I admired that she, too, a single mother, was giving life a good go.

Simona became very close to a male reader we had at the store who foolishly told her that she had a psychic gift and that she should be doing readings professionally. He also included in that conversation how much cash money she could make herself whilst still collecting the single mother pension. Simona was so excited that she messaged me early one Saturday morning to tell me that all of a sudden, she was psychic and because our male reader told her so, then it had to be true. Of course, she asked for a job as a reader in my store. I replied that it takes a lot more than just waking up to find yourself psychic and that perhaps she might like to do some casual work on the retail floor instead, and we will see how she goes from there. Simona was jumping with joy as she kissed and hugged me expressing the words I hear repeated over and over by every other psychic in my industry, "I love you, Rosie, you are my sister."

It was four days into Simona's first week at Embrace, and it was payday. Our accountant was ill that day, and therefore the wages were not paid. I sent a generic message to all my readers and staff, letting them know that their pay would be 2 days late as we needed to include the public holiday in amongst that. Everyone was cool and understanding except for Simona. Beautiful sweet Simona, who practically raised me on a pedestal that I had nowhere else to go but fall. As Colin would always remind me that the problem with expectations is that it always sets us up to fail and in Simona's case I had failed her miserably.

Answering her phone call that afternoon with a "Hey hun, how are you going?" I was blown away by her reply.

"You fucking bitch. You are not going to pay me. I hate people like you. It's because of people like you that I have had to live in my car many years ago." Her abuse went on and on until I had enough. I can't help but wonder if it was because she had to wait 2 days to receive her first paycheck or whether it was because I actually stood up to her and reminded her that I was the boss to whom she was talking so harshly to. Either way, she left, and the magical guru she portrayed me to be once again became a big unethical, unfair boss who didn't pay her staff. Another block and delete so she wouldn't know that I knew that she is now practicing somewhere in another state of Australia as a psychic and a healer whilst earning a pension from the Australian government. It doesn't take long for word to get out amongst my industry.

A few weeks after that horrible payday shenanigans, Simona had been treated for schizophrenia, and the voices she was hearing in her head became the basis of her elaborate psychic medium career.

It also didn't take long for me to develop a reputation of an unspiritual, unfair boss who was mean to her staff and treated them all so unfairly. I knew the truth, but the truth is whatever they see, and it usually goes to somebody who is pushing an agenda. You will always find that the lie is much more preferable than the truth, so it is always in their best interest to lie because it would mean that otherwise, they would be found out as a fraud. In their eyes, someone like me, who was not afraid to call it out for what it truly is, became an obstacle in their new lucrative shonky scheme.

It didn't take me long to realise that sadly, quite a few of my readers had an agenda. May I reiterate, not all, but a few. They expected me to build their business up, which I did, and then without any notice, leave and go into direct competition with Embrace. Like I said earlier, I don't believe in competition, and I am fully aware that the Universe provides for us all, but I do not believe in being sneaky, calculating, sly or dishonest about it. I worked as a team, they worked solo, and so it made my vision of embracing love and light into this world a much harder destination to achieve.

When we refurbished Embrace, it was a very different look from our original store. I wanted a more modern twist on spirituality, and my aim was to establish crystals as home décor accessories. It was a wild move as the spiritual community wasn't ready for that just yet. However, I knew our customer base was, so once again, I made a business decision and a very good one at that. We put a modern twist on crystals and turned our store into a "trendy" place to be.

On the day of our new opening, another psychic from a nearby store came to wish us luck. As she congratulated me on the new store and the amazing beauty that was in it, I saw her face change from the face that I knew to a face that reminded me of those zombies in Michael Jackson's "Thriller." With that came the foulest stench I had ever smelt, and the smell lingered in the very corner she was standing in. What was even more bizarre was that other staff members could smell it and also customers who automatically thought there was an issue with the sewerage pipes within the shopping centre. Even my husband, Ross, could smell it, and he doesn't even believe in all this hocus pocus stuff! In every basket, there is always one bad, rotten egg, and that particular day, it was her.

I called up Janine a few days later when even our strongest aromatherapy sprays were just not removing the stench. What was even more strange was that not everybody could smell it, and I did call our maintenance manager just in case it was a sewerage problem after all. The only thing he had to say is that our shop was nowhere near any sewerage pipes or drains, and I had to accept what I already knew. Janine did some pretty heavy anti-juju kind of magic, and even that wasn't getting rid of the smell in any kind of hurry. Eventually, Janine spent a week on removing it, and it never came back ever again. You see, jealousy rears its ugly head even amongst the spiritualists and I became hated for willing to take a big risk and just doing it.

We once had a psychic who was a little bit quirky around the edges. Her readings were good, and she would get booked out very quickly on her day. My only problem with Rochelle was that she would come to work dressed like she had just gotten out of bed. I had to address this with her on a few occasions, and when she started to show up like she was on her way to the beach, I really needed to put my foot down. There is nothing wrong with the boss wanting it her way, and all I wanted was for my staff to come neatly dressed for work. I drew the line at flip-flops on her feet, and she promised she would never wear them to work again. I must admit, for some time after that awkward conversation,

Rochelle came in dressed as she best could. Then came the sudden trips to the bathroom halfway through her readings, leaving her client alone in the room wondering when on earth she was coming back. On one occasion, I had to physically take myself to the bathroom to make sure she was OK, and she would always return to her client with a detailed description of her bathroom activities just whilst she was taking their hand to read their palm. I seriously wanted to die the first time it happened, but when this became a regular occurrence, I couldn't help but wonder how on earth would any other employer put up with this.

My final straw was during a reading, she asked the client if she could stay in the room whilst Rochelle went out to do her grocery shopping for her dinner that night. I very nervously asked the client where Rochelle was when I noticed the door open for quite some time and the client was sitting in the room like a stunned mullet. On that, she asked for a refund as Rochelle had pulled out a banana during the reading and had started to eat it. Of course, we refunded the reading, but I wasn't having someone as unprofessional as Rochelle represent my business. We had to fire her that day after she came back from her grocery shopping, and once again, I was blocked and deleted and the world's worst boss. I wonder if these people had real jobs in a 9-5 world, how would they ever survive, or better still, how would their employer put up with it all?

Being the big mean boss isn't always easy. I do hurt, and I do feel that sting of betrayal each and every time. It never does get any easier, it just gets more predictable. I absolutely fell in love with Marilyn. She was not happy in her previous retail job, so I asked her to come work for me at Embrace. Marilyn was jumping with joy, and we became good friends outside work. Sometimes her young kids would come to work when Marilyn had no babysitter, and I would take them for milkshakes and cupcakes and get them to put prices on all our small tumble stone crystals in return for a few stones for themselves to take home. I trusted Marilyn with the banking, and my personal emails, and I also trusted that my business would stay between the two of us. It didn't turn out that way.

Marilyn's background is in the healing modalities, and she was very territorial of anyone who would visit Embrace and also claim to be a healer. On one Autumn morning, I met a new friend who had just migrated from

London to Sydney, and I was excited to introduce her to the girls at Embrace in the hope she could make some new friends here in our country. As soon as Marilyn found out that Linda was a Reiki master with a very busy online presence, not only did she become quite rude and abrupt to Linda, she then reported her to the Reiki association to try and have this poor girl's business closed down. I knew there was a dark and jealous side to Marilyn, I had seen it with the way she had bullied another new staff member, but I didn't think she could stoop this low. In fact, Marylin, along with another reader Silvana, were so unaccepting of a new Indian healer who came on board they refused to call her by her name and instead referred to her as "the black girl." Well, that just got my back up and infuriated me to the point of no return. Not only is any form of racism against every moral fibre of my being, but who did they seriously think they were preaching healing, peace, and crystal energy when their beliefs were the opposite.

A few years back, Ross and I finally ticked a big tick off our bucket list, and we took our family away for a whole month to America. The first stop was of course Disneyland, followed by a road trip to San Francisco and then a flight to

New York, finishing in Vegas. It really was the best time of my life, and we took that trip with not a care in the world. Ross and I had worked our butts off that Christmas to make this trip happen. We hardly saw each other in the 7 weeks of Santa's Little Painters, and I worked up to 15-16 hours a day, every single day for a little over 2 months. My feet hurt, and they bled but I still kept going. The only sunlight I saw during those weeks was that coming from the shopping centre's skylight. We paid for our trip with our hard-earned money, and not a cent of it was used on a credit card. It is an amazing feeling of satisfaction, and the memories and photos I have will be forever etched into my soul.

I knew once I had landed in LA that Marilyn was not happy. She made it very clear that she did not find it fair that I had left my business for a month and that she was left to look after it. Mind you, she was getting paid well. We also had a massive debriefing before I had left in order to make sure everything was still going to be in order whilst I was gone. I really wanted nothing more than to enjoy my holiday with my family, but Marilyn made sure that each and every customer that came through Embrace's doors whilst I was away had heard how I had left my shop and left her with all the work to do. She was not appreciative of the gifts I brought back for her and her children from overseas. Instead, she had the hide to tell me to my face that she did not like them and that she refused to let her children eat American candy.

To make it up to her (and I'm still wondering why), I brought her a stunning $80 ring I knew she was eyeing off in another shop not far from ours. I thought it was the least I could do to let her know how much I had appreciated her looking after my business whilst I was away. The ring was received with lots of thanks, and that afternoon, I also gifted her a book from Embrace's shelves that I knew she really wanted.

It was not until the next day that it came to my attention by some of our psychics that Marilyn was promoting other psychic readers who did not work for Embrace on her personal Facebook page. It did not take a rocket scientist to know that in any other employment, it was a sure-fire way to lose your job. When I had mentioned that as a representative of Embrace, it really wasn't cool to be advertising other psychics other than the ones she worked for, that is when the gates of hell broke loose. Marilyn resigned on the spot, and I know in my heart she had to go. She thought by giving me no notice, it would really hinder my hopes of finding another replacement immediately, but you know what they say, in business, everyone is replaceable. The one-day setback with her became my comeback, but it took me a while to realise it.

I once again became the greedy bitch who treated her staff badly. Word got out this time far and wide, and I was accused of telling my staff what they could and could not do on their personal social media pages and leaving them to work whilst I travelled the world. The gossip went viral, and all I could do was scratch my head and wonder how on earth these people could not see what they were doing was wrong. I even had a fifteen-year-old working for me who could see that, and Marilyn was almost 50! Another block and delete, but this time it came with many others blocking and deleting me as well.

I was hurt. The story had been misconstrued, and all I asked my staff for was a bit of loyalty. Nothing more, nothing less.

I don't think I cried as much as I did after that. I felt like a fool, and for the very first time, I started hating my shop and the industry I was representing. Eleven years is a long time to work the way I had at making something so beautiful, and instead, it was becoming ugly. Against Ross's advice, I messaged Marilyn four weeks later, mentioning that it was Easter, and in the true nature of Easter, I would like to ask for forgiveness and move on from whatever it was I had done that was so wrong. I never did get a reply. I still feel her hate, yet I know that my family holiday to Disneyland was the catalyst for Marilyn to feel threatened and resentful of me.

I sunk into a deep depression. Not because I had felt guilty but because I think it was the final straw. I couldn't understand people, and the malicious gossip that was coming back to me was eating me to my core. This time I didn't call Colin, or Helen or even Janine. I sunk further into depression until I could no longer get out of bed. For weeks I cried over all the staff who had been so disrespectful and ungrateful for the incredible opportunities Embrace, and I had given them. Of course, Marilyn went on to start her own healing business on the back of Embrace's clients, and I do wish her well, even though I can't help but wonder that deep down, she too had to have known that what she had done was very, very wrong.

The snakes always show up when the grass is low, and it is during your hard times when they are revealed. If even the hard times are there in your life just for the snakes to show their true colours, then I guess it is something that is worth going through in the end. I learnt this the painful way when staff stole from me in order to set their own businesses up on the back of my skirt tails and when they thought that it was OK to send my customers to their own private practice because they sold the same products cheaper, or use my database in order to send details of their next up and coming workshop that didn't involve it running from Embrace. The very same staff who preached about karma were the same ones who stole stock and money, and they also stole time, claiming a 9-5 day with no breaks, but they found it OK to talk to friends for hours on end during my time, the time I was paying them to do a job, or taking long two-hour breaks and lying on their timesheets that they only had 30 minutes. In the end, I always became the unethical one because I had caught them out.

I was called unfair and unspiritual because I did not want to pay my staff for sitting down all day doing nothing, and when I asked them to dust shelves or move stock around,

I became the big bad wolf. The gossip amongst the girls was more than what you have heard in a school playground, and the bullying towards each other became out of control.

It became my fault if somebody had to wait an extra 10 minutes for their lunch break because the shop was full of customers and we just couldn't leave the shop unattended, or if they wanted to act like spoilt princesses instead of spiritual warriors and I was too hard on them. So instead of the employee becoming the victim of harassment and discrimination, the tables turned, and as my kindness started to get used against me as a weakness, I finally snapped and fired them all.

I realised that even the moon and stars needed the dark to shine, and I wanted to be the most sparkly shining star out there. For that to happen, I knew that the greatest tragedy when you are down is to stay down, so I got up, and I refused to let these people change me. I continued to be the kindest boss, but I also had to be the hardest. I am compassionate and empathetic, but as the boss, I also sometimes have to be one step ahead and a little savvy at times. Even though I work in the light, I understand the dark and know firsthand what it is like to live in it.

291

I, too, had my lessons to learn in all of this, and I realised that being spiritual did not always mean I had to be kind to others who were abusing me and my business that I had built up over the years. Being the boss means that you have to open yourself to being the bad guy in the eyes of your employee, and you need to keep remembering why you started all of this in the first place.

Sometimes I crumbled, other times I needed support, and many times I failed, but I never gave up on the dream of knowing I was to leave this world a much better place than when I first entered it. I still see nasty innuendos about me on social media, I still hear untrue gossip about me, and I still taste the bitterness of hatred and jealousy from people I thought were my friends, or worse still, from people who don't even know me at all. It is always in times like these that I would remember the words of the famous Steve Irwin: "Crocodiles are easy. They try to kill and eat you. People are harder. Sometimes they pretend to be your friend first." And wistfully, this is the spiritual world I began to understand.

I stopped trying to be everything to everyone and trying to make people happy because it was a game I was never going to win. People stopped liking me once they stopped getting their own way. Full stop! Once I started to walk in my true purpose, it somehow created fear in people, especially those who were coming from their ego. And so, one of my biggest lessons started to unfold, and for the first time, I let go of wanting everybody to like me. I voiced up when I wanted something done in my business, I stopped allowing people to run it their way, and I stood my ground. For that, I became a bitch, and a damn good one too! I stopped apologising for being where I was, and I acknowledged that it was a really cool place to be. It was here when the people who meant to represent Embrace showed up, and I have never looked back since.

My loyal legend staff, who have stood by me since 2010 when Embrace was birthed and who still stand by my side, believing in the dream as much as I do, have become an even stronger force than when we had first started. I have learned to sit with warriors where the conversations are always different. Some days I woke up a goddess, and some a cruel boss, and some days a fragile mess of both. It depended on whose eyes you were looking through and what their true agenda really was.

I knew from a very early age that I was born to do

something. I also know that every one of us was born to do something too, something that has a purpose. I believe that we all have greatness within us (and let's face it, mine is not in the singing field), and this greatness creates goodness that gives us a responsibility to manifest it into something wonderful.

I had my dream with Embrace, and I had to work on it. I also had to work on myself in order for me to go for what was mine in the Universe. Looking back at the people who let me down, betrayed me, and turned on me in the vilest manner, I came to understand what it meant that life is like an onion, and you have to peel it one layer at a time. Because sometimes you will cry, and cry I did. Nobody would have known that from my exterior that I showed the world or from my social media posts. However inside, I felt the pain of betrayal and realized that I had many Judases in the so-called spiritual world.

I also realised that this happens to everyone who has a dream, and it took me a long while not to take it personally. I lay in bed many nights asking God, "Why did this happen to me – again?" Why am I being slapped around, taken advantage of, used, and abused? It wasn't God who replied with the answer. It was my husband, Ross, with his simple words, "Suck it up, Princess."

Some people I believed in with my heart and soul who would be there to support me didn't come through, they turned on me instead, and I got ripped off. I knew in my soul that things were going wrong, but I couldn't go with them. An old manager stole my database with 1000s of names and email addresses in order to start her own spiritual business behind my back, and I was bummed. Life had let me down, and it wasn't fair.

I still knew I had a burning ambition to do something special even after I had tasted defeat, and I managed to find that power within me to look up from the position I was in, laying on my back; there was nowhere else to go but up. A metaphor of Christ's crucifixion if I had ever experienced one. In all of this, I had created within myself a comeback power.

Helen very wisely and sternly lectured me on taking ownership of my life. She would always remind me that nobody could live my dream but me. She asked me not to give myself permission to live a small life because I wasn't going to be able to fit my big dream into it. I took a deep look at the fakeness in my industry, and I realized at that moment that being on the bottom was overcrowded, and so from that day on, I strove to be the best I could be, with my God-given gifts.

I had to take myself to the very beginning and reach inside myself to feel that calling in my life I felt so strongly for all those many years ago. "I can do more, and I will do more," and with that, something in my heart caused me to get dressed and show up time and time again. I did exactly that, and I held my head up high whilst I did it.

I became hungry again and did things that my staff, who so badly wanted to be in my position, wouldn't do. I invested in myself with mentors, teachers, classes, workshops, prayer, and meditation. So, whilst my staff and psychics stole business from underneath me to start their own, I went that step higher and learnt and listened to the people who were doing something at a much higher level than I could have possibly been able to do on my own. I surrounded myself with quality people, and if truth be known, most of them were not in the spiritual industry or called themselves spiritual people.

I also made a firm promise to myself that because of a few bad eggs, I would not change the way I was as a boss. It would not be fair to the true and loyal staff, and so instead of becoming tougher, I became more loving and more accepting. I no longer allowed my staff to make me feel bad for the things they did not have in their lives. If I bought a designer outfit, I no longer hid it in order to not make others at work feel uncomfortable. If I wanted to go for a three-hour lunch break with an old friend, I did it instead of staying in the store so my staff didn't feel uncomfortable. In the mornings, I was just so tired I just couldn't get myself out of bed. I stopped feeling guilty for not coming to work. I no longer allowed my staff to steal my thunder and take away thirty years of standing on my feet with no holidays or days off, working till all hours in the morning, not spending precious time with my children to feel guilty anymore. I worked hard for it. I deserved it.

To get up from the canvas of life, I had to do things others wouldn't do in order to have the things tomorrow that others won't have, and I no longer allowed anyone to make me feel guilty for that.

My staff still get treated with respect and love, and my beautiful store is still a family environment. Just like in all families, there are some siblings who squabble or do not get on at times, mine are no different. We do kiss and make up, and we do love what we do.

If old staff want to call me unethical because it took me thirty years of hard work to be where I am, then so be it. If they want to question my time off whilst they are working being left with "all the work" to do and being paid well for it, then so be that too. If I need to remove some psychics from our store because they are not great readers and it leaves a bad reputation for Embrace, then that is what I need to do. I will no longer apologise.

As much as this might sound like a cliché, the haters thought that they would bury me but what they didn't know was that I was a seed. I found that these staff members formed a pack, sort of like a gang in a way, and it was Colin who told me that the reason they were running in packs was because they were weak all by themselves. It made sense once I was able to make sense of the lens I was looking through.

The thing about a seed, no matter what kind of seed it is, is that seeds can only grow in the dirt and that, my friend, is where Embrace grew to the big fat tree it had become.

Don't get me wrong, I don't want to make this sound like it is an easy thing to overcome, especially when your staff try to bury you in lies and false accusations simply because they did not get their own way in your business. Lies that I supposedly did what I did not do, assassinating my character that I always worked so hard to keep clean, celebrating, smiling, and gossiping about any of my misfortunes, but they had no idea that the dirt they were burying me in was the training ground for my growth.

Sometimes in your life, when something looks like it is the end of the road, when people have done you wrong, when things are just not going according to plan, you need to realise that instead of this being a burial, it is actually a planting instead. It is much easier said than done, but now that I have done it, I can sit on the top branch of the tree and see how far I had to climb. I know firsthand how hard it is, but there is something quite liberating once you have the understanding of where this needs to lead to for your life, your business and life's plans.

I found that a lot of people drawn into the spiritual industry, whether it be as readers or healers or those working in the store, tend to be narcissists, gaslighting, blame-shifting, and non-accountable personalities, who had me to a point where I felt like I was coming into work in the twilight zone. I seriously had to laugh at my last manager's words, who, just as she left, said, "You will never find somebody like me!" Oh, good God, I hope I never do!

You will find a lot of people in their own business will always complain about their staff being the main problem they have. Please don't get me wrong, I have had and still have some amazing, wonderful, admirable, talented, remarkable, awesome, brilliant and phenomenal staff that have worked at Embrace. Some needed to leave because they had bigger fish to fry, some because they had other careers to follow or studies and families to pursue, but these are the same people who I would have back in a heartbeat if they ever needed a job ever again, and they know it too! And with a cheeky smile on my face, the very ones who never deleted or blocked me! They know who they are!

In the words of Edmund Burke... "The only thing necessary for the triumph of evil is for good men to do nothing." I will continue to do my work with compassion and grace and strive to set an example for doing the right thing, always walking in the light as I do, and wearing my big girl panties at the same time!

Chapter 13

Are You a Good Witch or a Bad Witch?

"The line dividing good and evil cuts through the heart of every human being."

- Alexander Solzhenitsyn

"Are you a good witch or a bad witch?" Glinda asks Dorothy in "The Wizard of Oz." "Who, me?" Dorothy replies, "I'm not a witch at all; witches are old and ugly." Pointing to Toto, Glinda responds, "Well, is that the witch?" While Dorothy might be confused about Glinda assuming that everyone's a witch, I'm certainly not. Everyone is a witch when it comes down to it — it's merely a matter of harnessing the magical powers that bubble up from within and what road you wish to travel.

Let's go for a walk down the yellow brick road, shall we? As a very young girl (who watched the movie repeatedly, I may add), I always felt there was a spiritual connotation to the storyline. I remember being all but nine years of age and thinking that the yellow brick road can't be the only path to travel. There had to be another way, and so I spent the rest of my time here on this planet looking for it, sometimes finding it and at other times getting lost.

There seems to be a little bit of Dorothy in all of us, and that is why I believe we can relate to her so well. As she struggles against the dark forces along the path, and as she goes through the dark night of her soul, finding knowledge, courage, and love along the way, she is able to advance spiritually and become one with God, The Source, the Goddess. In Dorothy's case, it was the Wizard himself who represented the God force in all of us. As a nine-year-old to realise this, I look back at how far spiritually advanced I was as a child in a world that was still so blindfolded and in the dark.

At some point in time whilst watching the movie, I decided to make it my aim in life to be like Glinda the Good Witch. As much as I tried, I found there was a little bit of the bad witch in me too. It was just a matter of which witch I chose to be. I had a choice, so I chose the road, the yellow brick one, like most of us do. I found that on the yellow brick road, some days I was a good witch while some days I was a bad one. Both dualities existed within me, and it was just a matter of which one I wanted to entertain.

You see, you cannot have the light without the dark, the calm before the storm, the day without night, fire without water, heaven without hell, the yin without the yang, and salt without pepper. Once I understood this, it was there in the total darkness that I began to see the stars and understand the greatness of it all.

If we look at the work of the Swiss psychiatrist Carl Jung and his Shadow Work, it could help to understand this. Jung claims that you cannot better yourself until you first become conscious of your shadow. The shadow, he says, are the parts of ourselves we choose to repress or hide that we don't like about ourselves. We do that by pushing them down into our unconsciousness, usually during childhood, and we don't even know we have done it. Examples of our shadow aspects are selfishness, aggressive impulses, being extremely self-centred, arrogance, shameful experiences, and all the fears that we have and harvest. Jung states that these aspects lead to the certain types of behaviours that we see in certain types of personalities.

I have personally witnessed this where psychics and healers act with judgemental behaviour amongst their clients or peers. Many a time, I have heard a client being spoken about after they left their reading, when in fact, the very same psychic exhibits the same flaws. Another example of this is the entitlement pandemic. I call it a pandemic because it seems to be rife in this day and age, more so than in any other generation. I just need to look at my 14-year-old daughter, and I rest my case. It seems to me that the majority of readers I have worked with also have this mentality, mainly because they believe it within themselves that they are entitled because they have something, a special gift, an extra party trick that nobody else has. Judging people unfairly has also been a common trait. I have been in many a lunchroom during a psychic event where the readers gossip about their clients and are so unreasonably judgemental and harsh. At no stage have they ever looked in their own backyard before they started to throw stones into glasshouses. The problem with these people is that the moment you say something that is not in agreement with them, then that becomes their moment to play the victim, and drama galore follows. This is what I mean when I talk about the shadow. We all have it; it's just a decision we make each and every morning when we get out of bed regarding which path we wish to follow.

Don't get me wrong, the dark is just as important at times as the light. Lord knows I have personally been through many dark nights of my soul. Many mornings I woke up and couldn't bear to leave my bed because all I could think about were the mistakes I had made or how I could have changed things so the outcome could have been different. I felt some of the worst feelings in my life while I was in the purification process and, on some occasions, those which were the most painful ones.

Developing any kind of spiritual practise, anything that increases your awareness of yourself and your relationship to the world around you, is akin to stepping into a fire and letting the flames consume you whole. It's not gentle at all. It even appears to be unkind. There is rage, fear, and fury in the air. There will be days when you feel unable to move or, at times, even breathe. In these moments, it's difficult to see how there's anything else to do but let go, to surrender. I cannot begin to tell you how many times I have been on my knees begging the Almighty for a different outcome. It wasn't until I was down there on my knees that I decided it was time to stay there and surrender and allow what I need to grow and expand to come to me. It was here where the miracles lay. And that is precisely when it begins.

We seem to know that, no matter how venerable our guru or favourite practise is, most of this route is to be walked alone after an initial period of flocking to the light like a moth on a warm summer evening. They are not disturbed by darkness because they recognise that being human is a mixture of light and darkness.

Because we tend to view mistakes as obstacles to success, we are often thrust into situations that keep us from experiencing what we are looking for. In other words, the Emerald City. Life is going to spare us. She'll insist that we be present, and she won't baby us either.

As humans, we all have the Wicked Witch of the West in us, just the way she existed in the Land of Oz. In occult terms, the West is seen as a place of darkness and evil when the sun sets in the west and makes the world dark. The west is also seen as a way of darkness and ignorance, as both Adam and Eve were driven from the Garden of Eden to the west, and Satan approached them from the western gate of Eden.

Since Dorothy's house fell on the Wicked Witch of the West's sister, Dorothy had no choice but to fight the Wicked Witch on the dark side. We all know how the story goes, Dorothy after many battles, eventually throws a bucket of water over the Wicked Witch of the West, melting her into oblivion. It was here that the Wicked Witch of the West dissipated into nothingness as Dorothy courageously battled her demons and won.

You will find that in many religions and spiritual writings, consciousness and spiritual purity is represented by water. That is why you will see water represented as purification, protection and healing from a spiritual perspective for our friend Dorothy. So once the water washed over the Wicked Witch, Dorothy then gained her power, glory and enlightenment.

During the story of The Wizard of Oz and throughout her travels, Dorothy is constantly cautioned against straying and going off the path. While life is always an evolving mixture of good and evil, darkness and temptation lie in wait at every turn and tempt Dorothy to deviate from where she wants to go, which of course, is the Emerald City where the wonderful Wizard of Oz lives. Are you relating so far? How many times in your own life has temptation, ego, jealousy, greed, hatred, and spite stopped your journey to a better you?

Dorothy meets with some crazy friends along her journey, who we all can relate to at times. The Scarecrow, lacking in brains, is a part of all of us when we don't think before we act. Many times, in business and personal decisions, I have messed up because I was too spontaneous, I didn't think through properly, and when quite frankly I just didn't use my brain, instead letting my heart take away the moment like the wind on a gusty autumn day.

The poor ol' Tin Man, who didn't have a heart. As an empath, I don't really relate to the Tin Man too much. My heart has been my biggest blessing and my biggest downfall. But you know where I am going with this, and there have been times when we switch our hearts to love and kindness and do not receive it in return. And then we meet everybody's favourite, the Cowardly Lion. There is a huge wimp in even the most courageous and strongest people on this planet, and yet as they use every bit of courage they can muster, they forget to use their brains and heart along with it.

These guys were Dorothy's friends, the friends we have in all of us. The time when I didn't use my brain and instead made a silly decision that could have ruined me if it wasn't for my heart and courage to turn the whole situation around for the better instead of giving up. The times I didn't use my heart, and I retaliated when another psychic was being mean to me, and even though my brain and my courage in doing so gave me a feeling of winning, I felt awful once my heart found its way back to where it belonged. As for my courage, well, what can I say, other than I should have found the courage many years ago to write this book if I were not afraid to speak my truth. But once I aligned my brain and my heart, the words began to flow like a river with nowhere to go but forward.

And so, to understand our way in life and get back to our destination along the Yellow Brick Road, we must use Dorothy's three lost friends as a guide. In other words, if we want to be guided safely on the Golden Path of the Soul, we must have the secret attributes of these three main characters.

Begin by locating the Scarecrow in you and acquiring the requisite brainpower to realise where you want to go. With the morality, principles, understanding, and intelligence that you have, you can steer clear of the dark side and head in the right direction. More times than I would like to admit, I have worked with psychics and healers who have not shown any of these traits, and they wonder why their business is not thriving, why they have not found the love of their lives or why they cannot scrape up $2 to buy themselves a cup of tea. Like I said earlier, every single one of us is guilty of this. It is in repeating it over and over where the problem lies. In other words, they are not using their brains at all.

To find your creative inspiration within yourself, you must find the Tin Man within you in order to awaken your spiritual heart to the guiding power of God, the Source. We all have that dormant Source of God within us, but once we activate it, I promise you the direct connection and experience you can have with the God/Goddess force is better than any drug you could ever take. Once you open your inner spiritual heart, love in all its glory will come into your life like a firecracker on heat.

I truly do struggle with people who preach love yet bitch, moan, and backstab each other. It saddens me to my core. We will never like everyone. It is a given, a fact of life that there are just some people we just don't like. Myself included. It is in our heart centre, once we learn to open it, we can accept, tolerate and have patience with the parts of them we cannot heal within ourselves.

Love comes into my life because I am love. My Tin Man within me only needs oil for the aches and pains that my aging body is collecting along its way to Crone-ship.

Be certain to find the Lion in yourself, and have the courage to follow your intuition, instincts, and sense of direction, and let go of fear. I certainly did this when I signed the dotted line in 2010 in a very prestigious Westfield Shopping Centre. I most certainly signed my life away, but I found the courage, as scared as I was at the time, to just do it, and have the faith that the rest would be looked after. I have never looked back. I have also found myself working with psychics and healers who do not have the courage to move forward, and because of that, they make stories up about their peers and colleagues that do. They place hexes and curses and voodoo on a competitor, bad mouth them on social media or to anyone who wants to listen, and because of their cowardliness, they bring a tall poppy down to the point of sadness and hurt.

And finally, we go back to Dorothy, and her fourth friend, who seems to helps her accomplish great things. Toto was her faithful and trusted pet who stayed by her side throughout the whole story. They were made for each other; they were their own spiritual family, the same spiritual family we have with our closest, trusted friends. Without Toto, Dorothy was not able to evolve into a spiritual being.

Every aspect of Dorothy's relationship with her dog Toto symbolises her spiritual progression and her evolving into a higher state of being that she could not have done without him. These are the Colins and Helens and Janines in our lives. The ones who will come to your rescue and even bite someone on the leg for you if they have to, just the same way Toto did when he sank his teeth into Miss Almira Gulch. And in return, the very same friends who stood by your side the whole time are the same ones you will pack up and run away with if you had to. The ones who don't just take you to the bus stop but instead, they ride that damn bus with you! Toto and Dorothy frequently spoke to each other, and when she was in danger, or when she couldn't see the truth, Toto would bark and warn her of the dangers ahead. Think about the Totos in your life, the ones who are not afraid to speak up if you are in the wrong or warn you if they think you may be in for danger.

Just a side note here, did you know that the word Toto means "it is complete and whole"? Toto's love for Dorothy is symbolic of the love that she has for the essence of herself as well. In a way, she was talking to herself, that part of your spiritual family you see as yourself.

The moral of the story here is that you can only see what you are looking for. Though what you see with your eyes and perceive through your brain might be correct, it may not be true. You are the only self that can 'see' by looking inward. According to the Yellow Brick Road, it is advised that you use your innate knowing as your soul heads towards its journey.

You can be deceived by your eyes; your intuition is often correct. We have to trust our instincts because we can use them to direct our career, our relationships, our lives in general, whether they are accurate or not.

Listening to your intuition and expressing the characteristics of the Scarecrow and Lion, you will gain an understanding of your inner self, and the more that you show kindness, creativity, love, and compassion, the more likely you are to reconnect with the Light of the Source.

I only wish more people who teach this actually practiced it as well.

Although Dorothy annihilated the Wicked Witch of the West, the light won and vanquished her ego's evil darkness, her dark side, and that part of her nature that fell for the things that were not good in her life. It was not until Dorothy felt the spiritual power of the Light guide her, she opened herself to its wisdom.

The White Witch of the North was named Glinda, who symbolises the light and an inner power. Attuning ourselves to the cosmic intelligence found within is always to our North. Progress represents the soul's evolution. Once Dorothy had conquered her darker side, Glinda helped her on her way on the Yellow Brick Road so she could begin her exciting journey towards the Light.

To be endowed and act like the childlike mentality of The Munchkins, who surrounded Dorothy at the start of her journey, is a very special gift if we can attain it in this life. Their brief, childlike presence, innocence, and playful demeanour is a symbol of the mindset we should have on the path to Light. This is why you will always see me around young children. There is no better company than that of a child, and I am not known as the favourite aunty in our family for nothing!

Dorothy now faces battling darkness and temptation on her path as she makes her long epic journey along the famous Yellow Brick Road. As you might have guessed, the Yellow Brick Road serves as a metaphorical representation of the course of life. All the twists and turns as we walk the path with a few surprises along the way. The modern metaphor of a tradition of an alternative philosophy known as the Golden Path. In Buddhist philosophy and Kabbalah mythology, the Golden Road is the route by which we ascend to God, our true Creator.

I believe Dorothy is the epitome of this golden path; she is us and the journey we are already on. Those who seek to balance ego and love on the left and perform selfless service from the heart on the right.

And of course, as we all know, the ruby red slippers Dorothy wore show us that if we click our heels three times, we can have whatever we wish for; that is the power of manifestation at its finest, if only it were that easy.

And finally, we have the Wizard, the wonderful Wizard of Oz! Like the rest of us, he, too, covered his true identity with what he did not want the world to see, his true self. The grand old wizard wasn't really a wizard himself, but everyone adored him and treated him like royalty. He wore his cloak, the disguise I see in so many psychics and healers I have worked with over the years, and yes, it is true that more wear it than those who don't. The wizard worked in his grandeurs of egos, big flashy lights, showing off at every chance he could get and making everyone around him believe that he was holier-than-thou and much more above everybody else. Oh, the spiritual industry, why do you continue to do this?

Once Dorothy's trusted and devoted friend, Toto, tore down the curtains, everybody got to see the wizard for who he truly was... just like every one of us in all his vulnerabilities, weaknesses, idiosyncrasies, and sensitivities. It takes those that are closest and dearest to us to make us sometimes see the truth.

So, the next time you idolise someone, worship a psychic or a healer, praise their name as if they were your saviour, or put them on the pedestal, just remember that it takes only once for the curtain to come down to show the world who they truly are. I can tell you, I worked, lived, and breathed behind that curtain for way too long, and I know exactly what goes on there.

Dorothy had the magic inside of her all along, all she needed to do was tap her magic slippers. Maybe its time people start doing the same, instead of giving their power away to another guru, sportsperson, celebrity, Reiki master, psychic, healer, life coach, who really don't have the brains, heart, or courage themselves to change another's life for the better when they can't get their own shit together.

If you remember, the Wizard of Oz gave the Scarecrow, Tin Man, and the Lion all certificates to prove that they had what it took, yet they too had the power within them all along, they just didn't know it, so they didn't really need those certificates after all. I use this analogy to describe the way many readers, healers, and psychic associations offer certificates. They are based on their own protocols only, nothing else, and quite frankly, don't mean a thing more than the paper it is written on. Think twice before you see a psychic of the year because it doesn't necessarily mean they are, or someone with loads of certificates because anyone and everyone can hand them out depending on the business agenda they are trying to push. If anything I have said, just remember me on the floor with my pole dancing certificate, and you will totally get my drift!

Everywhere we look these days, there is a plethora of stuff about positivity, self-help, yoga, green juice, spirituality, good vibes, the law of attraction, and anything and everything gluten-free and vegan.

Most of us associate these messages with spirituality and positive energy. I'm not going to argue, I do too. These messages are not only uplifting, but they also spread positive energy. However, the problem is we don't get the entire story, and once we log off or get ourselves back home from our one too many self-help workshops, many of us still feel incomplete, fearful, and insecure because all of these "influencers" and gurus appear to have it all figured out.

Do you want to know a little secret? None of us has it all figured out (unless, of course, you are a Colin). We'll never be able to capture the depth and fluidity of our lives in a single blog post or yoga pose. And, speaking from personal experience, there's a lot of muddle to go through before you get to the love and light section.

Gurus, psychics, healers, and the likes, are alluring because they seem to have all the answers and are still positive, no matter what. Once upon a time, I would have put a few well-known, self-proclaimed spiritual teachers on a pedestal and dismissed my own inner guru if I had followed them. However, having the opportunity to work alongside these guys, I quickly learned the truth.

Though I admire and honour everyone's journey, I've come to understand that I resonate with a genuine vibe, one of authenticity, not one that just helps people see the bright side of life without ever mentioning the dark side. I truly believe that a part of Embrace's success, and as a reader myself, was because our clients can always relate to us; we are "normal" in their lives. I, for one, will be the first to admit that I spend my school mornings usually yelling and screaming at the kids getting ready for school and breaking up fights, surrounded by a shit load of dirty dishes whilst scoffing down a cold cup of coffee before even sitting down to say my prayers or my meditation. There are some days that the latter doesn't even happen. As much as Ross and I are madly, deeply in love, boy do we have some big fights. Thankfully, not very often, but when they happen, the whole street will know about it. We are human, and that is what humans do.

I have had to fail my way to success many times over, and even then, I am not always 100 per cent sure what success is supposed to look like. I admit I don't have it all together all of the time, but I choose my path and which road I prefer to travel. Inspiration is not found in the ones who are always happy or proclaim that they have all the answers. Those who share their struggles are the ones who inspire me the most.

Reciting positive mantras and drinking green juice whilst in a downward dog position is simple, but the real change occurs within. Once you expose the darkness, then love and light can enter, and when darkness comes again, you will be fortified to meet any challenge. The light will always help you find your way home.

There is definitely no shortage of celebrity and TV psychics, gurus, shamans, life coaches, and healers who are repromoting the same techniques and ideas that those who came before them hundreds of years ago were also using.

Instead, they are just rehashed ideas and refurbished to fit the modern world. Those that we see today have blurred lines between their good intentions and the con artistry they are working with. How much do you really know about these "special" people, the ones with all the answers to make your life a better one? If you take a real good look at their past and present, it is not at all what it seems. Their true narratives are of failed business dealings, frauds, domestic violence, a poor mindset around money, relationship difficulties, paedophilia, sexual perverts, and of course, lots of certificates to boot. In other words, grossly exaggerated achievements.

The first pattern we must acknowledge in the industry is that our audience is vulnerable. They are struggling with relationships, finances, illness, and at times just searching for answers. At this level of vulnerability, it is obvious that critical thinking and planning are the golden keys, but our emotions tend to cloud our decision-making abilities, and the bait is set once a promise to change our lives with very little effort is made. It is no wonder people keep coming back for more and more.

Go a little further down the rabbit hole, and you will soon realise that your preferred guru is not the person they portray themselves to be.

So in saying all of this, I just want you to remember that next time you give your power away to someone you believe has more brains, heart, and courage than you, someone who claims to have the secrets of the Universe that somehow you missed out on, or to someone in the name of healing who says they can fix you with a swish of their magic wand, I want you to remember one thing that it is all smoke and mirrors my friend. Just like the grand magical Wizard of Oz, it's all smoke and mirrors!

Chapter 14

You've Got a Friend

"Some believe that it is only great power that can hold evil in check. But that is not what I have found. I found it is the small things. Every day deeds by ordinary folk that keeps the darkness at bay."

- Gandalf – Harry Potter

I once heard a story about how God gave his Archangels weapons because He knew that they couldn't fight evil with tolerance. In other words, we do not, nor should we, put up with something if we know deep in our hearts that it is not right. I have a choice to either fight for what I believe is right or accept what I know is wrong, which is many times the easier way out. However, I made a choice many years ago in a year 3 playground surrounded by friends who were bullying another classmate, and I, a curly-haired, bushy eyebrowed awkward kind of kid, went straight to her defence. It was in the moment, faced with what seemed to an eight-year-old like a mob of a hundred men, that I knew I had the warrior spirit. I made a decision that hot summer lunchtime that I will continue to stand for what is right and make a noise even if I am the only one doing so alone. My intention was never to put myself as a guru or an expert in the world of spirituality. I am far from that and still have a lifetime of lessons to learn, but I will never cower down to the bullies. I will always stand for the truth. I am in deep gratitude for the opportunity of spending my last thirty years working alongside both the dark and the light, the goodies and the baddies, the cops and robbers, and anything in between. One of my biggest blessings has been some of the most influential people who have entered my life right at the time I needed them most. They taught me to be strong when it was easier to be weak, and they brought out my warrior spirit when I hid it for the sake of being ladylike. They also gave me the ultimate support, unconditional love and strong friendship bonds that I will forever cherish.

They say that we all come into this world with two families... the one you are born into and the spiritual one you find your tribe with, your spiritual family. I have a long list of people in my spiritual family, and they deserve every bit of appreciation and acknowledgement.

"I have come as light into the world, that whoever believes in me may not remain in darkness" John 12:46

My very own Mr Miyagi – Colin, my adopted grandmother and fairy godmother Helen, my teacher and good witch of the south Janine Donnellan, and my media coach Sharina Star. I thank you all for teaching me so much and giving me great role models to learn from. You have all kept me grounded and sane and reminded me when to breathe. Thank you.

My Embrace family, you all know who you are! You guys were with me from the very beginning and supported me all the way through. You are all my real sisters who have been there with me every step of the way and have been by my side the whole time. You have all had my back and have proven to the world that we all can agree to disagree and still live with kindness and compassion. I don't think I have ever laughed as much as I have in my whole life with anyone other than you guys, nor have I cried as much either. We have celebrated each other's success, we have mourned and grieved with each other during times of loss. We have all been there for each other while our babies were being born. We have all, at some point in time, been on the phone at all hours of the night supporting one another when no one else would understand the craziness of our lives. I thank you for being loyal to Embrace from the day we first opened, for the beauty you have brought to it, and for sharing the dream of a better world through it. But mostly, I thank you for knowing that whenever my back was turned, I never had to worry that any of you were ever carrying knives. You guys have all been the humblest and yet talented workmates I have had the pleasure of working with.

Embrace held its own, but to have you in my corner is what has kept the shop alive and kicking. You have displayed courage, stamina, humour, and loyalty, and for that, I will be forever grateful. I value our friendships, our nights out, dancing till we drop, and the mutual respect we all have for one another. Some of you were Embrace's glue during our early days and have gone on to do some amazing things in your own right, and the rest of you are stuck with me! I am so proud of each and every one of you, where you all are today, and the mark you are leaving for our future lightworkers. I truly love and adore you all.

A special thanks to Angelina and Lara and all the beautiful souls who have represented Embrace.

To all the brilliant and talented psychics, mediums and healers I have had the pleasure of working with over the years, and all the ones I have not met. All very talented in your own rights, and all wanting to make a positive impact on the world. I appreciate you all for who you are and the honesty and integrity you all display in our industry. You know who you are! A big thanks to Lisa Williams, Scott Alexander King, Trudy King, Maria Carr, Celestina Bishop, Debbie Malone, Rael, Alana, Effie, Dianne, Kerrie Erwin, Rick Mora, Saginaw Grant, Penny Sumbati and Willow Saige for reminding me that we can all work together separately with no competition or rivalry. I love you guys and what you all stand for. There are so many more I could name, but that needs to be saved for another book... so watch this space!

My parents, Anne and Mike – Embrace would not be still standing if it were not for the support of my parents. Endless nights when my twins were still babies, my parents would take charge and take over the babysitting duties. When I needed to work seven days a week, my parents were there the whole time to support my career and give me the space to do what needed to be done. I would not be where I am without either of you. I love you both more than I will ever be able to express. Thank you for putting up with a weird child and teaching me about hard work, morals, ethics and integrity. You are both the epitome of those words.

And finally, my husband Ross Pirillo, who will always be my number one fan and the love of my life. I found you my soulmate when I wasn't looking, and what a journey it has been ever since. The support you have given me as a sceptic in the world of psychics has been phenomenal, the love you provide has been overwhelming and the four extra children you have brought into my world has been one of my biggest blessings. You have always been my soft place to fall when I have cried, whinged, sooked, and moaned. You have been my hero and knight in shining armour as soon as somebody has been mean or cruel, yet you have also been my harshest critic. Always pushing me because you saw a fire in me that I didn't know was burning, and you had faith in me like I was a mustard seed.

You are the most incredible man I have ever known, the best father in the whole entire Universe and the world's best soccer coach! ☺ You brought me back to reality at sausage sizzles, showed me that there was more to life than the other side, and gave me joy that only the luckiest woman in the world would understand. I love you, babe. You will always be the glue to my glitter! ♥

"And In the End... There is only light."

– Rosie Shalhoub

About the Author

ROSIE

The girl with a big heart and a massive vision!

Rosie, the founder of Embrace, was given a vision at a very young age. She always knew that it was part of her destiny to create an environment of love, peace, harmony, and beauty that would be shared by many. Rosie comes from a place of authenticity, courage, and wisdom on a mission to transform lives for the better in a dynamic environment motivated by passion, unity, friendship, and a spirit of adventure.

The energetic spiritual entrepreneur is a true believer in the sacred feminine. With the roar of a lioness, she is a hopeless romantic, living in a world of make believe, fantasy, humour, and love. Embrace is that world!

Born with an incredible psychic gift who can communicate with spirits, Rosie has always blamed "it" on the gypsy in her soul. A free spirit with a sense of adventure and an attitude for fun, her style has always been quirky and cheeky mixed in with a whole lot of passion and love. Although Rosie claims to be stuck in a time warp of the '80s, her youthful attitude has granted her popularity amongst the millennials, teenagers, and her favourite of all humans... the children!

Embrace's success has a lot to do with Rosie's down-to-earth attitude and easy approach. With a background in paranormal psychology, strong psychic ability, and great passion, Rosie has forged a highly successful psychic career leading up to launching Embrace in 2010.

Embrace is a place of beauty and wonder, spiritual awareness, love, and peace. Rosie's main aim was to bring people from all walks of life together as equals. Through fun, joy, and laughter, she has managed to do this beautifully, creatively, and exquisitely. Inspired by her favourite song, "Imagine," by John Lennon, Embrace became that world.

Recognised as an inspirational entrepreneur, she is also the founder of the wildly successful Santa's Little Painter's franchise, which opened in the early '90s. Specialising in intricately hand-painted Christmas ornaments with seasonal pop-up shops throughout the country, the phenomenon of the business quickly became a huge success. She has dubbed herself "the woman with balls" in both the Christmas balls and crystal ball worlds.

Rosie is an internationally acclaimed author and the runner-up in the "Best First Work for an Author" by the International Tarot Foundation known as the CARTA awards. She has been featured in The Huffington Post and published in Successful Women in Business. She has also co-authored The Wellbeing Book and a coffee table book, "The Book of Inspiration for Women," which includes writings by inspirational women from all over the world.

As a regular on Sharina Star's Psychic Encounters on 2UE each Sunday night, Rosie quickly became known across Australia as one of the country's favourite psychics. She acknowledges with much pride her mentor, teacher, and friend Sharina Star for her foot in the door of radio land. She has also been featured on Smooth FM and various other radio stations across Australia and the U.S.

In 2014, Rosie and her husband, Ross, founded the widely successful "Festival of Dreams," a three-year project at the Hordern Pavilion in the heart of Sydney. Here, Rosie found international recognition working alongside Hollywood movie stars, Native American chiefs, our country's Indigenous elders, and well-known inspirational speakers. The festival gathered over 100 exhibitors in the mind, body, and spirit fields, with high-profile speakers, thousands of visitors, and the most acclaimed psychics, healers, practitioners, and speakers from around the globe.

In 2017, Embrace and Rosie joined forces in Embracing Rosie, an award-winning, charming, funny, and completely unscripted eight-part reality show. Embracing Rosie gave us all an insight into the life of Rosie, Ross, their family life, and her beloved Embrace. Currently screening on Aurora TV, the show will have you in fits of laughter and moments of awe.

These days you can find Rosie on TikTok as The Stoned Queen. A testimony to the crystals and gemstones she has so passionately based her career on.

Rosie lives in Sydney with her partner Ross, her twins Joey and Ellie, and her stepson Dion. She is a mother, lover, daughter, sister, friend, entrepreneur, teacher, artist, writer, speaker, visionary, dreamer and believer.

Rosie loves helping people connect with their best selves and explore their spirituality.

Facebook: Rosie Shalhoub Official

Instagram: Rosie Shalhoub

TikTok: The Stoned Queen

YouTube: Embrace TV

Email: contact@embraceaustralia.com.au

Website: www.embraceaustralia.com.au

THANK YOU

Please share your experience and leave review by simply scanning QR code.

h10.us/e3LLfX

Printed in Great Britain
by Amazon

15154225R00200